# SECRETS OF CONFIDENT COMMUNICATORS

## 50 Techniques to Be Heard

Diana Mather

I would like to thank my children, Leonie and Oliver, and my grandchildren, Sasha, Pierre, Raphaelle, Harry and Ben, as well as my son and daughter-in-law, François and Luci, because I always seem to writing something when I stay with them! I would also like to thank my editors, Jamie Joseph and Sarah Chapman, for their help and patience, my agent, Charlotte Howard at Fox Howard, and my partners at the English Manner, Alexandra Messervy and Gary Laverick.

# SECRETS OF CONFIDENT COMMUNICATORS

## 50 Techniques to Be Heard

**Diana Mather**

First published in Great Britain in 2014 by Hodder & Stoughton. An Hachette UK company.

First published in US in 2014 by The McGraw-Hill Companies, Inc.

This edition published 2014



*British Library Cataloguing in Publication Data:* a catalogue record for this title is available from the British Library.

Paperback ISBN 978 1 473 60027 0

eBook ISBN 978 1 473 60029 4

*Library of Congress Catalog* Card Number: on file.

10 9 8 7 6 5 4 3 2 1



Typeset by Cenveo® Publisher Services.

Printed and bound in Great Britain by CPI Group (UK) Ltd, Croydon CR0 4YY.

Hodder & Stoughton policy is to use papers that are natural, renewable and recyclable products and made from wood grown in sustainable forests. The logging and manufacturing processes are expected to conform to the environmental regulations of the country of origin.

Hodder & Stoughton Ltd

338 Euston Road

London NW1 3BH

www.hodder.co.uk

# CONTENTS

This SECRETS book contains a number of special textual features that have been developed to help you navigate the chapters quickly and easily. Throughout the book, you will find these indicated by the following icons.

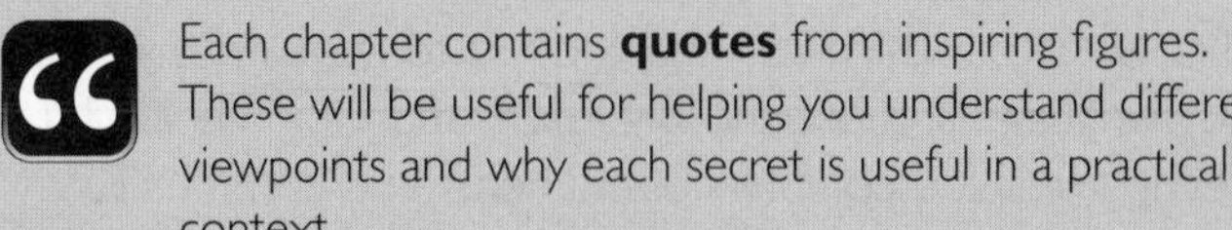

Each chapter contains **quotes** from inspiring figures. These will be useful for helping you understand different viewpoints and why each secret is useful in a practical context.

Also included in each chapter are a number of **strategies** that outline the ways you can put this secret into practice.

The **putting it all together** box at the end of each chapter provides a summary of each chapter, and a quick way into the core concepts of each secret.

12
13
14
15

You'll also see a **chapter ribbon** down the right-hand side of each right-hand page, to help you mark your progress through the book and to make it easy to refer back to a particular chapter you found useful or inspiring.

# INTRODUCTION

Who am I to be telling you how to become a confident communicator? Well, I have been around quite a long time and I have survived the ups and downs that life has tossed me. I trained as an actor, which has enabled me to develop my voice, use body language and expand my imagination for the work I do now. Acting gives you confidence and helps you communicate with other people, something that is vital in life. After leaving the world of TV and radio, I founded Public Image in the mid-1980s as a company specializing in image building, public speaking, speech writing and interview and presentation techniques. My work brings me into contact with all sorts of different people in various countries around the world, so I have had to learn to have the confidence to fly on my own and meet people I don't know in strange cities around the globe. It is fun and exciting, and as I grow older I find I have more confidence and life is more exhilarating.

In 2005 I began to offer training in international etiquette and modern manners, as I realized that these essentials were sadly missing in public, business and private life. In 2013 Public Image merged with The English Manner to form The Etiquette Connection and we now have offices in China, India, California, Russia, UAE, Kenya, Ghana, Nigeria, Tanzania and Mauritius. Our clientele has expanded to include businessmen and women, parents, students, teenagers and children, as well as politicians in Trinidad & Tobago, senators in the state of Jersey, first ladies from Nigeria and members of various royal families. I come from a family of four and have two children, five grandchildren, many nephews and nieces and many great-nephews and nieces. I am lucky because I believe a close extended family has helped me understand youngsters and enabled me to help them gain confidence and self-belief.

The aim of this book is to give you hints and tips on how to communicate in a wide range of situations with a whole array of different people. True confidence is something we should all strive for. We are born optimistic, with the confidence that we will be fed and cared for, but that confidence can be sapped as we grow older: our families, school friends and colleagues can all help drain as well as build our confidence and self-esteem as we go through life. The secrets in this book will help you overcome fears, complexes and self-doubt and give you the tools to communicate with confidence. I have covered topics ranging from style, dress, networking, public speaking, managing meetings, customer service, the media, talking to children and entertaining, to name but a few.

Because first impressions are very difficult to change – it is said that we make up 90 per cent of our minds about someone within the first 20 seconds of meeting them – we must make sure that the first impression we give of ourselves is the one we want to give. If we give an unconfident first impression, it then becomes difficult to create a confident image. Whether you like it or not, the way you look influences the way you are perceived and received by others. Police reports all describe people's dress, size, shape and colouring, because these are the first things people notice. We all have an idea of how the world sees us, but do you ever stand back and analyse the impression you convey to others?

Because so much of the way we judge and are judged today is visual, how you look has an enormous impact. You have to decide what image you want to impress upon people and try to make sure that you achieve it. But it can be difficult. If you are starting your career, you might not be confident, yet, about what your image actually is. If you have spent the last seven or eight years bringing up children or being out of work, then you might have lost confidence when it comes to going for a job. The secrets in this book will give you the confidence to write a CV, help you decide what questions to ask at a job interview and give you advice on what to wear. It's important to look the part. Think of the impression you are giving a prospective employer. The way you dress, speak and walk, and even the way you eat, all help to build a picture of you, which is equally true if you are going for promotion.

But what is confident communication and why is it important? It is obviously important in the world of work, but it is equally essential for your social life. To be a confident communicator you should transmit competence, reassurance and responsibility; your effect on the people you meet should be immediate and positive. This does not mean wearing power suits, but it does mean dressing with style and care; it means knowing the social graces, it means being prepared for any situation because you have done your homework, it means knowing your strengths and weaknesses.

A positive, confident image starts the minute you get up in the morning, and it is as much a matter of attitude as anything else. The way you react to other people builds up an image. Try and think of the effect your actions and reactions will have on others. Show that you care, not only about yourself, but also about other people. We have to show respect for others, which in turn brings respect for ourselves; the greatest gift anyone can give a child is self-respect and the ability to communicate well.

However strong your message is, if you can't get it across, it is lost. What papers and magazines do you read? It is not as easy to converse on any level if you don't read widely. Nobody expects you to be a political analyst or an expert on the economy, but if you are among a group of people and you cannot contribute perceptively to a discussion, it doesn't do much to enhance your confidence.

It is amazing what effect a really bright smile can have. It can light up a plain face and, more importantly, break down the invisible barriers that exist between us all. A smiling face is an appealing face, giving an impression of confidence. A good, strong smile is therefore a winning asset, so don't be afraid to use it.

Our expressions can also have a material effect on the way we think and the way we feel. Some psychologists claim that different expressions affect blood flow to the brain, causing positive or negative feelings. Laughter and smiling are said to increase the flow, producing positive emotions. Laughter, too, is strong medicine, helping us to achieve a natural high and a release from tension. That is why some people (especially children) laugh when they are nervous or in trouble. It is said that a single minute of laughter can give up to 45 minutes of relaxation, enabling the body to unwind. Happy people not only appear more relaxed and confident – they usually are! Communication comes from the face and the eyes, and a person's attractiveness is down to their expression, not the way their features are arranged.

This book also offers advice about talking to teenagers, who can be one of the most difficult groups to communicate with. In order to get on their wavelength, you need to think the way they do. Think back to when you were a teenager yourself and put yourself in their place. What was important to you then and what did or didn't you like to do? I know I was besotted by music, certain film stars, as they were known then, the Rolling Stones and Elvis, as well as my ponies! I didn't have to work to earn pocket money but I had to do jobs round the house and I hated being asked to do things when I was trying to listen to the Top 20 – we didn't have portable music devices in those days! Of course, every teen is different and you have to respond to and communicate with each individual in a different way. For example, some teenagers will want to go out a lot or spend money on clothes, so they will be motivated to get a job at the weekend or in the holidays. Others might prefer to stay in bed half the day during vacations and weekends.

It has now been proved that teens need plenty of sleep, so don't moan every day if your children won't get up. (If they are up half the night listening to music or hanging out with friends, that is quite another thing!) It is a fine line between giving them a structure and nagging – see Secret 47. If you can provide a private space in your house that can act as a haven for your children and their friends, you may not be exactly sure what they get up to but at least you will know where they are and be able to check out their state of health and generally keep an eye on them. This can also reduce the potential for battles with them and provide more opportunities for communication.

If you are an employer, it is vital to be a confident communicator. Employees need to be sure of what is expected of them, so you need to be clear and concise when you carry out induction. It is also essential to have written guidelines so that everyone knows what their job description actually means. This is especially true of nannies, au pairs and anyone else who works in your home. Misunderstandings can easily occur if the number of hours and the tasks specified are not completely understood, which can happen especially if you are employing someone whose first language is not English.

To communicate confidently, you have to know what your body is saying; you have to understand your 'body talk' and that of other people. Negative signals are the ones we usually transmit without being aware of them. Avoiding eye contact or looking round the room makes people look shifty. Look out for this in teens and children. Body touching is a comfort blanket. Shrugging shoulders and sprawling in a chair are two traits used by teenagers and they are often signs of unease within themselves which portray an 'I don't care' image, whether they do care or not.

People often show nervousness by rubbing their mouth, touching their cheek, biting or licking their lips or scratching their head. People who constantly clear their throats are often anxious or uneasy. So what are the positive signals we should be transmitting? Good eye contact shows that you are listening, as does smiling and nodding as this encourages others to open up and communicate. Sitting forward when listening displays a sense of stillness and confidence, and indicates you are in control of yourself and your situation. It sends out signals of tranquillity and authority, which are also infectious and can help to calm others; this is especially useful in any form of confrontation.

The main thing about confident communication is that you need first to have confidence in yourself. You *have* to believe that you can do what you set out to do. There is no room for self-doubt in this world if you are going to achieve success and happiness, in whatever forms they take for you. That doesn't mean the arrogance of believing you are always right but it means having the confidence to try new things, the confidence to fail and the confidence to forgive, in particular yourself. Once you obtain that bedrock of self-assurance, you will be able to communicate with the confidence that you will be heard.

# Start on the path to true confidence

*'Believe in yourself! Have faith in your abilities! Without a humble but reasonable confidence in your own powers you cannot be successful or happy.'* Norman Vincent Peale

*'Optimism is the faith that leads to achievement. Nothing can be done without hope and confidence.'* Helen Keller

*'The brave man is not he who does not feel afraid, but he who conquers that fear.'* Nelson Mandela

*'If you don't like something, change it. If you can't change it, change your attitude.'* Maya Angelou

*'I finally realized that being grateful to my body was key to giving more love to myself.'* Oprah Winfrey

To be a confident communicator, you need to have confidence. That goes without saying, but if you haven't got confidence to begin with, how do you get it? Confidence is something we all strive for because true confidence helps you communicate effortlessly and successfully. It comes from knowing and believing in yourself. That may sound blindingly obvious, but most people do not really know themselves or believe in themselves. Confidence is something we are born with but often lose as time goes by and life throws us its brickbats, so it is often a case of rebuilding what we once had.

Having true confidence means being able to rely on your own decisions and choices, to be able to make valid judgements without constantly having to ask the opinions of others – in other words, to have the confidence to determine your own future. It requires confidence to walk into a room and enjoy the fact that you won't know a single soul, or to wear what you want to wear and not worry about what others may think. Starting up a business or going for a high-flying job demands true confidence, if you are going to be a success. True confidence also means not being afraid of taking criticism or making mistakes and being bold enough to try something new.

It is true that, if you are dissatisfied with yourself, you will never be satisfied with life. For most jobs today it is vital that you radiate confidence because it denotes competence. It is the same in the social arena: having confidence will make people accept and admire you, and that will improve your private life. The following strategies will help you improve your confidence and help you achieve a new, positive outlook on life.

## EVALUATE YOUR SELF-IMAGE KINDLY

Today the image of physical human perfection shines at us from magazine covers, billboards and TV advertisements. Very few of us, however, measure up to these faultless paragons and this can be a major cause of unhappiness and low self-esteem. You have to be honest with yourself when you evaluate your image in the mirror, but you must also be fair to yourself and appreciate your good points. Most people are dissatisfied with at least some aspects of their own appearance, which is why so many people resort to cosmetic intervention, but that doesn't always create true confidence – sometimes the reverse.

Look at yourself as if you were looking at a dear friend who has asked you for an honest opinion. Be kind to yourself. We all have good points and you have to appreciate yours. You might have beautiful eyes, a noble nose, lustrous hair or a swanlike neck. Whatever your good points, start to appreciate them rather than wishing to be something you are not.

Of course, if you *can* do something about what you don't like, do it! Don't put up with crooked teeth if you can get them straightened and, if you want to be slimmer, go on a diet. A good haircut can do wonders to boost morale, so shop around and find a stylist who will take time to listen to you and help you try something new. Take a look at your wardrobe and decide what really suits you and get rid of anything you are not sure about. If you aren't comfortable in your clothes, you can never feel truly confident. Keeping fit will also help boost energy levels, which in turn will boost confidence.

## RECOGNIZE YOUR ACHIEVEMENTS

Do you talk to yourself? If so, how? Some people talk to themselves in a way that they wouldn't do to their worst enemy. I used to be one of those people. I have no sense of direction and constantly get lost in the car, with or without a satnav, and I used to call myself all sorts of names and tell myself how stupid I was until I realized that I was actually making things worse. I was eroding my confidence in even finding my own front door, so I had to reassess how I was valuing myself. I changed my attitude and started to treat myself with compassion and respect. Instead of criticizing, I started praising myself.

Try this exercise: look at yourself in the mirror every morning and tell yourself you are looking good and that it is going to be a good day. Before you go to bed, look in the mirror again and praise yourself for what you have achieved. Even if things have gone wrong, instead of letting it depress you and bring you down, discover what you can learn from the experience and tell yourself that you will do better next time. Do this for one month and you should feel more positive and more confident.

Write down any beliefs that hold you back. Where did those beliefs come from? When did you start believing those things and do they have basis in fact? So often, we believe things that are embedded in our minds during childhood. If you are constantly told you are not good at maths because your exam results weren't top notch, or you can't skate because you always fall down, you will lose confidence in yourself and never improve. If you want to do something enough, you can do it; tell yourself you can and have confidence in your own abilities!

**We determine much of our attitude towards ourselves and the world around us by what we think. Having a positive attitude helps build true confidence, so start talking yourself up and remember, confident people are sexy people!**

## MAKE A LIST OF YOUR GOALS

What would you do if you had the confidence to do it? Some people dream of travelling down the Amazon, learning to ski, writing a book, designing clothes, climbing a mountain or running a marathon, but they never fulfil their dream because they think it is going to be impossible for them. They say, 'But I don't think I could do it.' If this sounds like you, ask yourself why not. Provided your goal is realistic, you can achieve whatever you want to achieve, but you must have confidence in yourself and your beliefs and part of that confidence comes from self-respect, so celebrate your personality.

Make a list of the things you want to do and give yourself a timeline to do them. Don't worry if you don't succeed at the first attempt. Don't slate yourself, treat yourself with kindness and encourage yourself. Achieving a lifetime's ambition is one of the best and surest ways of giving yourself true confidence.

## Putting it all together

Be proud of yourself and appreciate yourself. You are a unique and special person; there is no one else in the world exactly like you, so be confident in your own individuality. Treat yourself with kindness and respect, give yourself praise when you deserve it and don't beat yourself up when you make a mistake. Use mistakes as learning experiences and don't let them erode your confidence in yourself. Remember:

- You have to love yourself for people to love you: self-assurance is both charismatic and compelling.
- Have the confidence to push your boundaries and try things you have always wanted to do.
- Mix with like-minded people and people with a positive attitude; try not to surround yourself with negative people who will drain your energy and self-confidence.

Look at people you consider to be successful and analyse what they have done to get where they are. Very few people are 'overnight successes' – so look at their journey to success and learn from them. At the same time, ask yourself what 'success' really means. Wealth and possessions don't necessarily mean happiness or fulfilment, and there are many other measures of success.

Don't make snap judgements about people and compare them with yourself, especially if they are very successful and you feel that you are not, as this will certainly drain your confidence. Have confidence in what you have done with your own life. Are you happy? Have you done your best? Do you have a good relationship with friends and family? If so, I think you can call yourself a success, so let that help you find true confidence.



1 2 3 4 5 6 7 8 9 10 11 12 13 14 15 16 17 18 19 20 21 22 23 24 25 26 27 28 29 30 31 32 33 34 35 36 37 38 39 40 41 42 43 44 45 46 47 48 49 50

# 2 Blow up the mental block

*'Most of the important things in the world have been accomplished by people who have kept on trying when there seemed to be no hope at all.'* Dale Carnegie

*'Don't play for safety. It's the most dangerous thing in the world.'* Hugh Walpole

*'I failed my way to success.'* Thomas Edison

*'Nothing matters very much, and very few things matter at all.* Arthur Balfour

*'Fortune befriends the bold.'* Emily Dickinson

Many people have a mental block about all sorts of things, but it is vital to get rid of these blocks if you are going to become a confident communicator. There are several reasons why some people would rather throw themselves under a bus than stand up and speak in public: shyness, worrying about what other people think, lack of preparation, anxiety about the level of interest in the topic and fear of being in the spotlight are just some of them. Most blocks start in childhood or adolescence, but a bad experience when first venturing into the workplace can also have a detrimental effect on confidence.

If you cannot blow up your mental blocks, they will inhibit your ability not only to speak in public but also to try new things and meet new people. We must always remember that we are all unique human beings with something unique to offer, but we sometimes have to dig deep to find out why we don't like doing certain things and then analyse the reasons. Let's look at the word 'fear' and take the fear out of it by breaking it down like this:

- False
- Entrenched
- Absurd
- Rationales.

Many of your fears are false and they become entrenched because you have thought that way for a long time. Some fears are absurd, although that doesn't mean they are any less real to you; but their rationale has no foundation in reality.

## WRITE DOWN YOUR WORST-CASE SCENARIOS

Writing things down is a good way to identify mental blocks. Think about all the things that make you say 'I couldn't do that' or 'I don't like that' and ask yourself why. Identify the things that frighten you or make you feel uncomfortable and start to analyse them. Do you like walking into a room where you are unlikely to know anybody? If you don't, why do you think this is? Do you like trying new experiences – different food, a new haircut, going to the theatre, a new sport? Again, if you don't, ask yourself why. If you feel self-conscious walking into an unknown environment on your own, examine your fears and write them down. What is the worst that can happen?

Write down your worst-case scenarios and read them out loud. Do they sound logical, do they sound frightening? If the answer is that you fear that no one will talk to you or that people will stare at you, saying this out loud will help put that fear in its rightful place, back in your childhood. If you won't try a new cuisine, you are missing out on the chance to excite and challenge your taste buds. If you won't change your image and try different styles, you will always be stuck in the same old rut, and if you won't accept an invitation to the theatre or to a clay-pigeon shoot because 'you know you won't like it', you could be missing out on a life-altering experience and a whole new circle of friends.

Writer's block is a different type of mental block that can cause feelings of fear and panic, especially if you have a deadline to meet. If you are writing an essay, an article or a speech and you simply don't know where to start, just write anything that comes to mind. It may be nonsense but the important thing is to get some words on to the screen or paper. Write whatever comes into your head about your subject and then leave it for a while. When you come back to it, you will usually find that you have written something useful. Keep this up until you have blown up your block.

## CHANGE YOUR MINDSET AND OPEN UP YOUR MIND

The reason a mental block stops you from being a confident communicator is because it stops you joining in. If you have never tried something, you cannot talk about it or share your experience with others, so not being able to enter into conversations can inhibit your ability to communicate fully with friends or colleagues. As I will discuss in the course of this book, good communicators have a broad knowledge of a wide range of subjects and take an active interest in all of them. So it is a matter of changing your mindset so that you become open to all opportunities.

Don't be afraid of what people might think of you. Somebody once said, 'You won't worry about what people think of you when you realize how little they do.' Have confidence in yourself and allow your mind to open up in the areas where you feel you have a mental block. You are always forging new neuro-pathways in your brain and by thinking positively about something that has been a negative for many years, you can eventually change your mindset – about anything. It is just a matter of thinking positive thoughts and telling yourself you can.

## EXPAND YOUR HORIZONS AND ENRICH YOUR LIFE

Yes you can! You can blow up your mental block and expand your horizons and begin to enrich your life. Good communicators are interesting people and they are interesting because they are interested. They want to know about life and what it has to offer and their minds are open to all possibilities. Once you have identified the issues that are blocking you from doing what you might secretly want to do, the next step is to see what is realistic and what isn't.

If you have a mental block about eating frogs' legs, that's fine, but don't let it put you off French food in general. If you have a block about playing golf because you think it is not for you, go for a lesson and, if you like it, have another one! When you next have the opportunity to go to a party or networking event, look forward to the opportunity of meeting new people, expect the best from them and walk into the room with a smile.

**Putting it all together**

To be a really confident communicator, you need to have an open mind. You need to unlock your mental doors and be receptive to all possibilities. You cannot communicate well with others if you are narrow-minded because you will have entrenched ideas and opinions about things that will preclude you from appreciating other people's points of view. So many people have closed minds and that is why there is so much conflict in the world. If we have deep-rooted opinions about different cultures and beliefs, for example, then we will never be able to understand or respect their views.

# 3 Beef up your self-image

*'Don't ask for an easier life; ask to be a stronger person.'* Kirsten Goeser

*'I define nothing. Not beauty, not patriotism. I take each thing as it is, without prior rules about what it should be.'* Bob Dylan

*'What one has not experienced, one will never understand in print.'* Isadora Duncan

*'Your true value depends entirely on what you are compared with.'* Bob Wells

*'To succeed, it is necessary to accept the world as it is and rise above it.'* Michael Korda

A positive self-image is a vital part of being a confident communicator. You have to love yourself in order to love others, so one of the things you need to examine is how you talk to yourself. We all talk to ourselves, whether we are aware of it or not, but if most of your self-talk is negative it will do nothing for your self-image. Talk to yourself positively and try to understand how your body reflects your state of mind.

When I am very stressed, with lots of international travel and deadlines to meet, never mind domestic issues, my heart starts racing, I get a headache and I begin to think I cannot cope. This starts to undermine my positivity. That's when I tell myself that it is quite natural to feel like this, as I have been rushing, not eating properly and worrying half the night instead of sleeping. I tune into my body and tell my heart to slow down and I ask my brain to get rid of the headache and, yes, this usually works.

My mother used to say that a problem is not a problem if it can't be solved; it then becomes a fact. Be realistic about what you expect to get done each day or each week. Learn to say 'no' if people ask you to take on more than you can deliver; don't let others erode your energy or your self-belief. Try to experience as many different things as you can, especially those things that you are afraid of. Think about a particular fear you have and how it would do wonders for your self-image if you were able to overcome it. Breaking such barriers will leave you feeling stronger and give you a real boost. You might long to learn to dive off a high diving board but your fear of heights holds you back, or take a degree but think you are not bright enough or that it is too late. This secret will show you strategies you can use to help you achieve your ambitions. Provided your ambition is not unsafe or foolhardy, go for it! It is never too late. What barriers can you break?

## EXPAND YOUR MIND

It's not easy to have a decent conversation if you read only celebrity magazines. Reading a serious newspaper or its online equivalent regularly, as well as serious publications such as *New Scientist* or *National Geographic,* will keep you informed of world opinion and events and give you facts about other current topics. If you are with people having a discussion on a serious subject, it won't do much for your self-esteem if you realize that you have nothing to contribute. I always say 'I know an awful little about an awful lot' because I like to be able to join in conversations about as many subjects as possible; therefore I read, listen to the radio and watch TV as well as going to the cinema and theatre as much as I can.

We all take in information in different ways. Some people need to see things, others prefer to hear information and some like to 'experience' to gain knowledge, so decide how you like to learn and start expanding your mind. This may seem hard to do when we are too busy or too tired to fit anything else into our lives, but swapping one type of activity for another doesn't have to take up any extra time. For example if you normally listen to music when you are in the car, try listening to a talk radio station such as BBC Radio 4 or BBC Five Live to keep up with current affairs and hear analysis from experts. Aim to read a serious newspaper on at least two days a week, so that you can gauge the truth behind the headlines and read about other views and opinions. Try not to have preconceptions about anything. If your opinions are based on fact or experience, you can be confident that you have something meaningful to contribute and that does wonders for self-esteem.

## DEVELOP YOUR SOCIAL SKILLS

Having courteous manners and good social skills will help raise your self-esteem. When meeting new people for the first time, it is imperative to use those all-important first few seconds to make a good impression. Smile! It's as simple as that. Smiling instantly makes you look warm and friendly and puts people at their ease. It is still correct to say 'How do you do?' by way of a greeting. This is not intended as a question, however, and the correct response is not 'Very well thank you,' but 'How do you do?' If this sounds a little archaic to you, it's acceptable to say 'Good morning', 'Good afternoon' or 'Good evening' or even 'Hello'. However, 'Hiya' or' Hi' is considered too informal for a business context. Never kiss someone on a first introduction.

When introducing people, it is still correct to introduce a man to a woman, a younger person to an older one and junior staff to senior staff in business. It is also a good idea, especially if you are the host at a social occasion, to give a snippet of information about the people you are introducing, to provide the springboard for a conversation. For instance, 'Susie Wells, this is Andrew Johnson. He's just moved into the area and likes to play squash. You're a member of the squash club, aren't you?' And it's always best to introduce people even if you find out that they already know each other. If you think that they might possibly have met, then, 'Tom, you know Nigel Briggs don't you?' will allow you to introduce them if they are not acquainted.

## RESPECT YOURSELF

If you don't respect yourself, you will not respect others, so it's vital to get rid of limiting or restricting beliefs about yourself that reduce your self-respect. There are various reasons why you might have these limiting beliefs and the main one is the way you talk to yourself. When the mind talks, the body listens, and you can talk yourself equally into triumph or disaster. By examining how you talk to yourself, you can discover whether or not your responses to demanding or challenging situations are balanced and positive or illogical and destructive. These habitual responses have a major impact on how you feel and how you operate.

If you want to feel good and be able to function as effectively as possible, talk to yourself in a positive manner and look for the positive in both situations and people. As you go through your day, check your 'self-talk'. Whenever you catch yourself thinking or saying something negative about yourself, about somebody else or about the situation you are in, find something positive to focus on. Being positive in outlook can dramatically improve your confidence and self-respect. Nobody is born a pessimist!

1 2 3 4 5 6 7 8 9 10 11 12 13 14 15 16 17 18 19 20 21 22 23 24 25 26 27 28 29 30 31 32 33 34 35 36 37 38 39 40 41 42 43 44 45 46 47 48 49 50

## Putting it all together

Try to broaden your mind and enhance your knowledge of as many subjects as possible. Read as much as you can and watch or listen to well-researched, trustworthy current affairs programmes to be able to have a valid opinion on what is happening in the world. Try to get rid of presumptions or prejudices and keep an open mind. Always smile when you meet someone. Say 'How do you do?' or 'Hello' when greeting and don't kiss on first meeting. Always try and give some information about the people you are introducing so that they have something to help them start a conversation.

Break new ground and try things you thought were impossible for you. Never think you can't do something or that it is too late. It is never too late, so don't delay, start something today – it will do wonders for your self-image. Treat yourself with kindness and learn to understand your body. Self-talk can be damaging if it is too negative, so check the way you talk to yourself. No matter how pessimistic you think you are, you can train yourself to think more positively. There are courses and books to help people find a more constructive frame of mind and they can work wonders. Feelings like revenge, jealousy, intolerance or negativity drain your energy and eventually only damage you. These feelings also show on your face. If you think positive thoughts, you will have a confident and positive expression, which is very appealing and attractive and helps you to become a confident communicator.

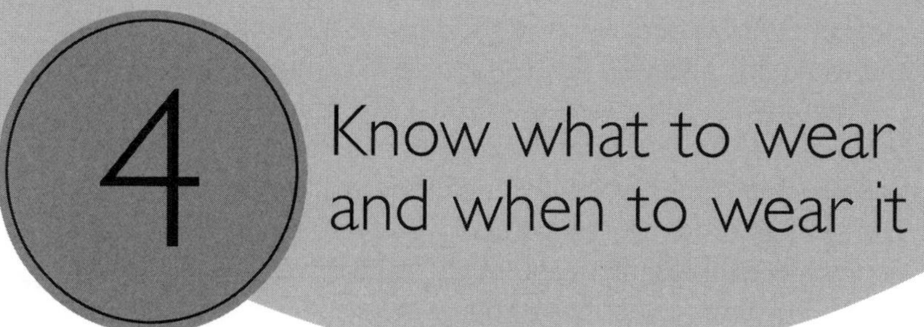

# 4 Know what to wear and when to wear it

9 10 11 12 13 14 15 16 17 18 19 20 21 22 23 24 25 26 27 28 29 30 31 32 33 34 35 36 37 38 39 40 41 42 43 44 45 46 47 48 49 50

*'I dress to kill, but tastefully.'* Freddie Mercury

*'There are moments, Jeeves, when one asks oneself, "Do trousers matter?"' 'The mood will pass, sir.'* P. G. Wodehouse

*'Eat to please thyself, but dress to please others.'* Benjamin Franklin

*'What is it about wearing a tuxedo, or that little black dress, that makes us feel confident, beautiful, splendid, even invincible?'* Vera Nazarian

*'There is no doubt a new dress is a help under all circumstances.'* Noel Streatfeild

It is important to know the dress code when we go to an event, especially if is a formal one. A friend of mine once came to a charity concert I was organizing but his wife had forgotten to tell him it was black tie, so he turned up in a suit. He had barely got through the door before he turned round and said 'We're going home.' This was a shame because it wouldn't have mattered at all, but when he apologized afterwards he said that he would have felt out of place all evening. This story demonstrates that one cannot underestimate the power of apparel.

The question of what to wear to a formal event can cause great anxiety, and if you are anxious you cannot be a confident communicator. In the mid-twentieth century most gentlemen owned their own full evening dress – white tie – but today most people will hire it from a good gentlemen's outfitters as and when it is needed. The only people who might still have evening dress in their wardrobes today are diplomats, some politicians and members of the royal family. However, it is worth investing in a dinner jacket if you go to formal parties or dinners. The same goes for morning dress if you go to many weddings because, if you keep hiring the outfit, you will have probably paid for it a few times over after a couple of years.

The reason why correct dress can lead to success is because you have shown respect for the person who has invited you to an event or function by choosing the right attire. Because the rules of society have changed vastly in recent years, it is easy not to bother but, if you want to get ahead, it is worth making the effort to get it right.

## WHEN AND HOW TO WEAR WHITE TIE

White tie is worn so seldom nowadays that it can cause panic when seen on an invitation. If the invitation says 'formal' it can mean 'white tie' or 'black tie'. White tie is known as 'full evening dress' and it is now really only seen at royal or diplomatic events and banquets. The double-breasted jacket is usually black but can be midnight blue, is never fastened and should show just a hint of the white waistcoat beneath. A white (hand-tied) bow tie is worn with a white, wing-collared dress shirt fastened with dress studs; cuffs should be double-cuffed fastened with cufflinks. The waistcoat is low-cut, in pique honeycomb and with a shawl collar. All buttons should be fastened save for the bottom button. Black tapered trousers with two pieces of braid running down the side of each leg and black patent shoes complete the ensemble.

Women should wear long dresses at a white tie event. These may be sleeveless gowns, or dresses with long sleeves. Long gloves (often white or toning with the colour of the dress) should be worn at all times, except when dining. Rings are worn under the gloves, bracelets go on top and closed-toe shoes are correct, with stockings or tights.

## WHEN AND HOW TO WEAR BLACK TIE

Black tie is now often the smartest form of dress that the average man will wear in the course of his life. Like white tie, it is just for evening occasions. The dinner jacket (tuxedo in American English) first came into fashion in the nineteenth century but its origin is hotly debated. The Americans will argue that it was first seen at the Tuxedo Club in New York, whose members decided that they liked the idea of something less fussy and formal than white tie. In Britain it is said that it was the Prince of Wales, the future Edward VII, who first wore a similar outfit to an event in Monte Carlo. Until then, men of the upper classes would have worn white tie every evening.

Black tie comprises the following items:

- A black or blue-black jacket, which can be single- or double-breasted with either notched or shawl lapels. A single-breasted dinner jacket should never be fastened
- Trousers that match the material of the jacket and are usually slightly tapered, with one braid running down the outside of each leg
- A white dress shirt with a turned-down collar, a marcella or frilled front and fastened with either buttons or studs. Cuffs should be double-cuffed (i.e. for cufflinks)
- A bow tie, which should strictly be black, hand-tied and made of silk
- Shoes in either highly polished black or patent leather

If you wish to wear a 'top pocket handkerchief', wear a white one. It should be worn in a plume shape, without the corners of the handkerchief showing. Waistcoats, which are optional and rarely seen nowadays, should be low-cut and only worn with a single-breasted jacket. A cummerbund can be worn around the waist instead and its folds should point upwards. This was originally to catch any crumbs if the wearer was rather large!

Women going to a black tie event should wear any dress that stops somewhere between floor length and just below the knee. The dress can be colourful: the object of the men wearing just black and white is so that the women will stand out. A clutch bag is most suited to these occasions and shoes should be closed-toe, although sandals can be worn in the summer.

1 2 3 4 5 6 7 8 9 10 11 12 13 14 15 16 17 18 19 20 21 22 23 24 25 26 27 28 29 30 31 32 33 34 35 36 37 38 39 40 41 42 43 44 45 46 47 48 49 50

## WHEN AND HOW TO WEAR MORNING DRESS

Morning dress is seen at Royal Ascot, race meetings, royal garden parties and some weddings. Despite the name, it can be worn at any time of day. It is not a 'morning suit' as the coat and trousers do not match.

Morning dress for men comprises the following:

- A morning coat or tailcoat: curve-fronted and single-breasted and in either black or grey. The coat is never fastened
- Trousers: usually charcoal pinstriped
- A white shirt with a turndown collar is correct, worn with a tie, although a high wing-collared shirt is often still seen at weddings
- A white, grey or buff/camel waistcoat
- Black lace-up shoes

Black or grey top hats are optional at weddings but compulsory in the Royal Enclosure at Ascot. For attendance at Ladies' Day at Ascot, a grey coat is de rigueur.

For women, formal day dresses can be colourful and made of varying materials depending on the season. A small clutch bag is correct here. Shoes may have a heel but anything over three inches is not practical for standing for long periods. Straw hats are permissible after Easter for women. The old rule still applies that hats are not worn indoors after 6 p.m. Fascinators remain a sartorial hot potato.

### Putting it all together

It is worth remembering that we make up 90 per cent of our minds about someone in the first few seconds after meeting them and that the first thing we notice are their clothes. Whether we like it or not, clothes set the scene for so many prejudices, so it is best to get things right. This includes making sure you know the dress code before you attend a formal function, so that you know exactly what to wear. Even in this day and age, it is still difficult to be confident if you see that everyone else is wearing black shoes with formal dress and you are wearing brown.

By all means show your personality by 'customizing' your formal outfit but, if you really don't like wearing a 'penguin suit', perhaps you will never be able to communicate confidently at that type of event. It might therefore be better to decline the invitation – but be aware of what you could be missing out on!

1 2 3 4 5 6 7 8 9 10 11 12 13 14 15 16 17 18 19 20 21 22 23 24 25 26 27 28 29 30 31 32 33 34 35 36 37 38 39 40 41 42 43 44 45 46 47 48 49 50

# 5 Dress for success

*'A woman's dress should be like a barbed-wire fence: serving its purpose without obstructing the view.'* Sophia Loren

*'You can never be overdressed or overeducated.'* Oscar Wilde

*'Marge, I can't wear a pink shirt to work. Everybody wears white shirts. I'm not popular enough to be different!'* Homer Simpson

*'If people turn to look at you on the street, you are not well dressed, but either too stiff, too tight, or too fashionable.'* Beau Brummel

*'We act the way we dress. Neglected and untidy clothes reflect a neglected and untidy mind.'* Anon.

Since clothes are the first thing we observe when we see people and they define our image even more than hair or faces, it is essential to be aware of the image we are projecting through our clothes. Whatever we wear, the clothes must be in good order, especially shoes. Shoes can say a lot about a man or a woman. If they are slightly scruffy when you go for a job interview, for instance, the employer's subconscious thought might be that, if you can't look after yourself, you can't look after the job. The same goes for your hair, nails and skin, which all go into forming your image, but do you know what it is?

Take a long, hard look at yourself and try to decide how you come across to the world, and then ask a couple of friends how they see you; it's often a shock to discover that others see our image as quite different from what we think we are projecting. Whether we like it or not, women are judged more by their clothes than men, and I for one like to make a fashion statement wherever I go! Because I run my own company, I can choose to a certain extent what I wear and the image I project, but that image must be based on reality. You cannot be confident if you are not happy in your own skin and if your image is not founded on fact.

## DRESS FOR WORK – WOMEN

The next task is to think about your height and body shape. Take a look in the mirror and measure your bust, hips and the length of your torso from under your arm to the waist, as well as your legs. Armed with these statistics, you will have a good idea of what size you really are. To be stylish, you don't need a fortune – you just need to give time, some effort and thought to the issue. Colour is important, so when you have decided on your colour range, buy clothes that will mix and match, because you can extend your wardrobe enormously that way. If you buy a pair of trousers, for example, you can choose them in a colour and style that will go with a particular jacket, sweater, T-shirt or blouse.

At work, make sure your style of dress suits your company. If the dress code is formal, it is still correct to wear tights (pantyhose) or stockings rather than bare legs. If you want to have bare legs in the summer, make sure your legs are in good condition. Don't show too much flesh – be it cleavage or leg; blouses and shirts should not be tight. If you are short, don't wear a long jacket as it will make you look smaller – and wider – and baggy or wide trousers will also shorten your overall image. Skirts should not be too short in the office and very high shoes or open toes are not suitable for office wear either. Choose colours that suit you, but be aware that some companies prefer muted colours.

**It is fine to mix and match colours and styles in clothes for work. There is no need to get stuck in a rut.**

## DRESS FOR WORK – MEN

Despite the fact that in many work environments today you may have more choice about what to wear than a suit, a suit is still what many men feel they must wear to the office. Suits originated in the seventeenth century in Britain, but it was not until the nineteenth century that the suit developed into something we can recognize today. It was Beau Brummel who revolutionized the suit, working with tailors in London to create clothes that followed the line of the body and fitted snugly – something never seen before in men's tailoring. He was concerned with silhouettes and single colours, shunning fancy materials and rich fibres, and what we know now as the lounge suit was born.

Suits should be grey or navy; although black has become popular, it can look a bit funereal. It is also worth remembering the old adage 'never brown in town'. The choice of fabric design for your suit is up to you. Stripes come in pinstripe or chalk stripe: the former is subtler and often the stripes are closer together than chalk stripe. Checks or plain are other options.

The jacket length is crucial and should stop just below the bottom. A good test to check whether a jacket is the right length is to place both hands at your sides and see whether the jacket stops in the palm of your cupped hands. On a two-button suit the top one should be fastened when you are standing; on a three-button only the middle button is fastened. All buttons are unfastened when seated. The buttons on the sleeves should have buttonholes and it is the sign of a good suit jacket if they do. Ask for working buttons or 'surgeons' cuffs' when selecting a suit. If you are short, don't wear a long jacket because it will make you look smaller. If you are tall, don't wear a jacket that is too short and make sure that the sleeves are long enough.

Trousers should 'break' (end/finish) over the first few laces of the shoe. Make sure that they are long enough, but beware of baggy or wide trousers, which will make you look shorter.

Ideally, long-sleeved shirts of good-quality cotton should be worn with suits. Choose colours that suit your colouring. Jacket sleeves should always be allowed to show 15 millimetres of shirt cuff. Shoes should be black for the office and belts should match shoes in colour.

Socks should be made of natural fibre – wool, silk or cotton. You can express your personality through your choice of tie on a day-to-day basis but, for serious business meetings, a darker tie is required. The tie should finish just above the belt/start of the trousers.

## USE ACCESSORIES TO RING THE CHANGES

Make as much use as possible of accessories to change the appearance of your work outfits. Changing scarves, belts and even buttons can give outfits a fresh look and save money too. It's appropriate for women to wear discreet jewellery, but not huge earrings, bracelets, necklaces or watches, which can be distracting. Jewellery is not usually appropriate for men working in a formal environment so, again, be aware of the size of rings, bracelets and watches. Men should avoid wearing earrings if possible.

Hats are not often worn these days but, in the days of universal hat wearing, customs developed based on showing politeness and respect. The old rules still apply:

- A gentleman never wears a hat indoors. This rule applies to beany hats and baseball caps as much as to more traditional headgear.
- A man should remove or doff (tip) his hat to show courtesy to another, such as when passing a woman or a man of higher status whom he knows in the street.
- Women should only wear hats during the day.
- Women may wear a hat that is part of their outfit indoors – indeed it used to be mandatory for a woman to wear a hat for church and other formal daytime occasions.
- A woman never doffs her hat to anyone.



1 2 3 4 5 6 7 8 9 10 11 12 13 14 15 16 17 18 19 20 21 22 23 24 25 26 27 28 29 30 31 32 33 34 35 36 37 38 39 40 41 42 43 44 45 46 47 48 49 50

## Putting it all together

Look after your clothes and they will look after you! Even if you wear a uniform and you don't have the daily problem of deciding what to wear, it is still important to take pride in your clothes:

- Keep them in good condition by hanging them on decent hangers with enough space for them not to crease.
- Make sure your clothes fit properly and check them regularly for marks and spots.
- Ensure that they are pressed and crease free.

To find the cut that will make the most of your particular build, you'll need to try things on. This is the only way to find out what flatters you most. It is as well to remember that, as we get older, our shape will change, so every so often take the time (at least half a day) to go into all sorts of shops and try on lots of different clothes. It is a good idea to put on things that you cannot afford as well as those you can, as it will help you gain a concept of quality and cut. Feeling confident about your image is an essential element of feeling confident enough in yourself, which is all part of helping you become a more confident communicator.

# 6 Build your brand

*'Don't compromise yourself – you are all you've got.'* Janice Joplin

*'We are what we repeatedly do. Excellence then is not an act, but a habit.'* Aristotle

*'Be yourself; everyone else is already taken.'* Oscar Wilde

*'It's lack of faith that makes people afraid of meeting challenges, and I believe in myself.'* Muhammad Ali

*'Example has more followers than reason.'* John Christian Bovee

Today everything seems to be branded, so why not build your own brand? If that seems a good idea, where do you start? 'Brand' in this context means the impression you make, the way you behave and the image you project. You need a powerful brand to reflect a positive image, and a positive image gives you overall confidence.

Building your brand starts the minute your feet hit the floor in the morning; it is as much a matter of attitude as anything else and you have to show respect for others to earn respect for yourself. Today the image of physical fitness and mental alertness is an important one to project, especially at work. A person's weight, for instance, can send out different signals. To some people, carrying a lot of weight says, 'This person doesn't take an interest in themselves or care what anyone thinks of them.' To others it might say, 'This person is obviously steady and secure in themselves.' The problem is that you don't know the effect your brand is going to have, so you have to be aware of all possibilities.

What goes into building a brand? We have talked about clothes and shoes because that is what people notice the minute they see you. A good brand needs good manners, and the following rules will reinforce your brand through these courtesies:

- Offer to carry a heavy bag or suitcase if you see someone having difficulty.
- Stand up when somebody enters the room.
- Hold a door open for someone coming through behind you.
- Offer an elderly person or a pregnant mother your seat in a train or on a bus.
- A man should settle his partner into a chair before sitting down to dinner and should also open a car door for a woman.

## BUILD YOUR OFFICE BRAND

Everything you use in your place of business – business cards, stationery, your business card holder and promotional material such as leaflets and brochures – must be of the highest quality in order to send out a confident message. Similarly, using a good pen says that you are worth dealing with because you value yourself and your brand. The same goes for your wallet, purse and watch. None of these should be ostentatious and they needn't mean you have to mortgage your house to buy them, but they should be the most expensive you can comfortably afford and be kept in good condition. The reason this is important for your brand is that it indicates that you care about quality.

In the Far East, especially China and Japan, the business card is seen as part of you. The quality of the card and how it is given and received can make or break a deal.

Handbags and briefcases need to be practical as well as attractive. They should be made of good leather and be of a neutral colour. Use a good cream to clean the leather and pack bags with paper when they are not in use to preserve their shape. Don't overfill them, as this will put a strain on buckles and stitching. Keep them tidy inside as well as out and replace them as soon as they begin to look worn.

## BUILD YOUR IBRAND

Your web presence must be professional. It is essential that your website be easy to navigate: there is no point in having the most dazzling looking website if prospective customers and clients can't find their way around it easily. On the other hand, it should also stand out from the crowd. People trawl the net and visit hundreds of websites, so try to make yours different. Here are some key points to remember:

- Text is more easily read on a white background, so resist the urge to make it different by making it almost impossible to read.
- Don't make your pages too cluttered: less is more when it comes to looking classy and upmarket.
- Keep the site up to date and change key words, images and videos regularly to keep the search engines interested.
- Use different web services to check how many visitors you have to your site and link to as many trusted, relevant sources as possible.
- Your logo is a vital part of your brand, so scrutinize it carefully; does it truly reflect your brand? Does your email signature include all relevant information?

## BUILD YOUR 'LOOK'

As already mentioned, a smile immediately builds a bridge between you and anyone you meet as well as making you look and feel confident and in control. A smile is therefore essential for building a good brand. It also goes without saying that being well groomed is vital, for the same reason. After clothes, clean and healthy-looking skin and hair are what people will notice about your appearance. Therefore, to make a positive first impression a good haircut is a must, as is hair in good condition. Nails must also be clean and well manicured.

The facial expressions you use show others what you are thinking, or what they *think* you are thinking, which can be quite a different thing! Be aware of your 'default' position when your thoughts wander and you stare blankly into space. I became aware of mine when I was a passenger in a car, mindlessly staring into shop windows. I caught a glimpse of a very unhappy face and thought 'Help – that can't be me!' But it was. I was unhappy at the time but I didn't want the world to know it, so I made up my mind to try to think happy thoughts as much as possible. The thoughts we think eventually show on our faces as emotion lines, so if you don't want frown lines and crow's feet, think positive thoughts and your face will have a positive, attractive expression.

If you wear glasses, make sure they suit your face as well as being trendy. The top of the spectacles should be in line with your eyebrows, and the bottom no lower than the top of your cheekbones. If in doubt, ask your optician for advice. Fashion glasses can make a statement and wearing glasses can be used to give an air of mystery but wearing sunglasses can create a barrier, so unless the sun is really bright it is better to take them off so that those you are talking to can see into your eyes. Have your eyes checked regularly by an optician as they are an early warning system for a number of ailments, glaucoma and high blood pressure among them. If you wear contact lenses, keep them really clean to prevent damage to the eyes.

Having good teeth is also vital for a strong brand. Crooked, yellow or missing teeth are unacceptable since the advent of modern dentistry. Cleaning teeth regularly with a whitening toothpaste will help keep them white, and other products are on the market that will also help lift the colour. However, don't go too bright white otherwise you could look as though you are sporting a lovely set of false teeth, which rather defeats the object.

## Putting it all together

As we have seen, the first things about you that catch people's eye are clothes, so they are a vital element of building your brand. To create your own designer label, analyse what you have in your wardrobe and decide what you want to keep and what to throw out by asking yourself these questions: 'When did I last wear it?', 'Why did I buy it?', 'Do I still like it?' Having decided what you want to keep, you might want to alter, revamp and accessorize favourite outfits to bring them up to date and make them unique to you. It is amazing what new buttons and a new collar can do to change and update a suit or jacket.

Your brand is also all your office 'tools', such as pens, stationery, business cards, wallet, watch, briefcases and handbags, so these should be the most expensive you can comfortably afford. Similarly, your website reflects your brand and so it needs to be both memorable and easy to navigate.

Your brand is you and should fit you like a second skin, so be honest and maintain your integrity. If you are not sure who you are, it is impossible to be a confident communicator, and building your brand is one way of finding and cementing your identity.

# 7 Find your style

*'Fashion changes, but style endures.'* Coco Chanel

*'Create your own style... let it be unique for yourself and yet identifiable for others.'* Anna Wintour

*'One should either be a work of art, or wear a work of art.'* Oscar Wilde

*'Simplicity is the ultimate sophistication.'* Leonardo da Vinci

*'Never use the word "cheap". Today everybody can look chic in inexpensive clothes (the rich buy them too). There is good clothing design on every level today. You can be the chicest thing in the world in a T-shirt and jeans – it's up to you.'* Karl Lagerfeld

What is style and why do we need it to be confident communicators? Stylish people are confident people because they know that they have taken care of their image and confident people communicate well.

The dictionary definition of style is chic, elegance, flair, grace or panache – and we need all of these to be stylish. The way you dress, the way you speak and the way you walk should all have a sense of style. Good grooming is essential, of course, but it's not just expensive clothes, it is the overall image of being appropriately presented, in an often-understated way.

In the past, correct etiquette dictated that we should not draw attention to ourselves by wearing ostentatious clothes, and this rule still applies in many business environments. Garments were to be of the highest quality and the best possible cut, but clothes were always to be unobtrusive. Fortunately, this etiquette is considered out of date today: we have only one shot at this life and we need to make our mark! That doesn't mean dressing in a way that is so extreme it makes people stare. Having style means wearing clothes that fit really well and wearing something that is bit different from the usual run, whether it's an unusual pair of shoes or earrings, an amazing belt or tie, a colourful T-shirt or a beautifully cut jacket.

To achieve style, you need to take the time to think about yourself and your image. It's not just a question of spending money: the high-street stores provide some really great clothes at affordable prices. However, it's always best to buy a few good things that will mix and match with cheaper items, even if you have to save up for them. A smart jacket, a well-cut skirt or pair of trousers and some good shoes will never let you down.

## WEAR THE RIGHT COLOURS

Wearing the right colours is also vitally important: colours that enhance your skin tone can make the difference between you looking healthy and vibrant or tired and washed out. The colours you wear should also reflect your personality. To make choosing the right colours simple, skin tones may be divided into two categories: warm and cool.

- **Warm people** have an olive or creamy skin tone, brown or hazel eyes and brown, black or auburn hair. Earthy, autumn colours suit you best – russet, fern or olive green, burgundy, butter yellow, scarlet, beige, air force blue, mid and deep brown.
- **Cool people** are those with pale or pink complexions and light brown, blonde or black hair and blue or green eyes. The spring colours are most flattering to this colouring. These are fuchsia, cherry, pink, vermilion, emerald and apple green, lilac, turquoise, light and dark blues, chocolate brown and navy.

These are just a few of the wealth of wearable colours possible for each type. Everybody wears black and white but, if you are pale, check that they don't drain the colour from your skin.

Wearing the right colours gives you confidence because they make you look good.

**For more information on the colours that will suit your skin type, make an appointment to see one of the many image consultants working around the country; they will be delighted to help.**

## WEAR THE RIGHT MAKE-UP

Your face probably receives more scrutiny than any other part of your anatomy – so it has to look good. For women, make-up, skilfully applied, will enhance your looks and make you feel confident that you are 'putting your best foot forward' through the course of your day.

Before buying a foundation, test it on your skin under the jawline to ensure that it exactly matches your skin tone. This goes for men buying a tinted moisturiser. Blusher is great to shade or shape the cheekbones and jawline, as well as giving added colour. It should be applied just under the cheekbones and taken almost level with the eyes. A subtle whisk of the brush under the jaw line can help definition. If you are blonde or grey, pink tints are best, while for strawberry blondes, redheads and brunettes, the coral and rust shades are more flattering. Olive and black skins often need little or no make-up. To conceal the odd pimple or hide bags under the eyes, use a concealer.

Good mascara is essential, so choose one you like and that goes on easily. Eye shadows are made in every colour and there are creams, powders and pencils, and again, personal preference is what counts. Keep eyebrows tidy, but don't over-pluck them, because after a while they will stop growing. If they need defining, use a brush with a matt eye shadow or a soft pencil. Use a lip liner to trace the outline of your lips and enhance your mouth shape, and to help keep your lipstick in place. There are lipsticks on the market now that really do last all day. Again, choose a lipstick to complement the colours you are wearing.

## PAY ATTENTION TO HAIR AND NAILS

Your hair should be your crowning glory, so use a good shampoo and conditioner and have a good haircut. Find a hairdresser who will listen to you and advise you on a style that will suit your face as well as the texture of your hair. Women – and men – with long hair who work in an office, especially in a senior position, should put up their hair or tie it back. As well as being clean, tidy hair is a must for both sexes so, if you have a problem, gelling your hair to make it smooth could hide unruly layers and split ends. If you colour your hair, don't allow your roots to show! If colouring becomes expensive and difficult, consider going back to your natural look.

Nails must always be clean and well looked after for either gender. Nail polish should never be chipped. False nails are useful if you have trouble growing your own, but they weaken the nails when you have them taken off and they need a lot of attention. Don't forget your toenails if you are putting them on display. If you go without shoes in the summer, keep your feet well scrubbed and use a pumice stone to keep heels smooth. Keep feet in good condition by treating them to a pedicure occasionally, and visit the chiropodist if there is a hint of a corn.

1 2 3 4 5 6 7 8 9 10 11 12 13 14 15 16 17 18 19 20 21 22 23 24 25 26 27 28 29 30 31 32 33 34 35 36 37 38 39 40 41 42 43 44 45 46 47 48 49 50

## Putting it all together

Having style will give you confidence and this confidence will help you become a confident communicator. Whether we like it or not, the way we look and the way we dress influence the way we are perceived and received by others. The way someone dresses or speaks, the way they walk and the way they eat all help us build a picture of them – positive or negative. There's a saying that 'People seldom notice old clothes if you wear a big smile.' While that might be true, having sense of style is important if you are to be noticed in this world.

Until recently, you could judge someone's job, their background and how much money they had by the way they dressed. This is now more difficult: some of the richest, most successful people are so eccentric that they don't care what sort of impression they project. However, that does not apply to most of us, and it's well worth taking some time to create your own 'look' and develop your personal, unique style by choosing clothes that fit well and have something special about them.

- Select colours that suit your complexion and that make you look healthy and vibrant.
- Look after your complexion and, if you wear make-up, make sure it enhances your features.
- Have a good haircut and choose a stylist who will work with you to give you the look you want.
- Keep nails spotlessly clean and manicure them regularly. Make sure polish is not chipped – and don't forget the toes!

# 8 Perfect your posture

*'Jane reminds us that God is in his heaven, the monarch on his throne and the pelvis firmly beneath the ribcage. Apparently rock and roll liberated the pelvis and it hasn't been the same since.'* Emma Thompson, *The Sense and Sensibility Screenplay and Diaries*

*'I'm really critical of my posture, it makes a big difference. And I try to suck my belly in. Everyone should do that, whether you're on a red carpet or not. Even if you're just going out to dinner with your boyfriend you should try and suck it in.'* Katy Perry

*'I'd love to look like my mum when I am her age. She taught ballet for years, and my attitude to exercise and fitness has definitely been influenced by her. She's 84 now, and I've watched how well she has aged, and a lot of that is to do with her fantastic posture.'* Sarah Parish

*'I want to get old gracefully. I want to have good posture, I want to be healthy and be an example to my children.'* Sting

*'Walk tall, walk straight and look the world right in the eye*
*That's what my mama told me when I was about knee high*
*She said son, be a proud man and hold your head up high*
*Walk tall, walk straight and look the world right in the eye.'*

Lyrics by The Popes, sung by Val Doonican

9 10 11 12 13 14 15 16 17 18 19 20 21 22 23 24 25 26 27 28 29 30 31 32 33 34 35 36 37 38 39 40 41 42 43 44 45 46 47 48 49 50

Everyone – men and women – should stand and walk tall in order to communicate confidence and competence. Most of us have no idea what we look like when we walk, but a good walk says as much about you as all the other aspects of your appearance. I realized that I needed to do something about mine when I was working in television and saw myself on camera – it was not a pretty sight! I was brought up on a farm with horses and spent most of my life wearing wellies, mucking out stables and pushing wheelbarrows; my father used to say I walked like a foreman on a building site. It took two modelling courses to get rid of my builder's gait.

Climbing the stairs is another situation where we seldom see ourselves. Since part of our brand of confidence is to look elegant and in control at all times, we need to learn how to walk up and down stairs in a way that exudes confidence. Here are some tips:

- Walk upstairs on your toes (this helps strengthen the muscles in your back), allow one hand to glide up the banister with you at hip level and look straight ahead. Keep your hand on the rail so that you can stop yourself from falling if you accidentally trip.
- When descending the stairs, let your hand move smoothly down the banister and keep your head up rather than looking at your feet. If people are waiting at the bottom of the stairs, look at them as you come down.

## STAND TALL

When I was at drama school, we were taught to imagine that a piece of string was attached to our head, reaching to the sky and pulling us up straight. I still do this now, and the result is that I stretch my back so that I can almost feel my vertebrae separating; I am sure they are not actually separating, but I feel much taller after doing this and my improved posture has cured all my upper back problems! So stand tall, pull your stomach in and try to stretch your spine. Your chin should be parallel to the ground so that you are looking straight ahead rather than at the ground. Keep your arms by your sides and your shoulders back but relaxed; don't force your chest out unless you are in the army!

Stand with one foot slightly in front of the other. This means that, if you are standing for a long time, you can imperceptibly shift your weight from one foot to the other while still looking elegant and alert. Comfortable shoes are a must if your job entails much standing. Many people have a cupboard full of shoes that are not really comfortable because sometimes it is hard to combine fashion with comfort. Don't be seduced into buying fashionable shoes unless you know you will be able to wear them on a regular basis.

## SIT UP STRAIGHT

It is just as important to sit tall as it is to stand tall. I do a lot of work in schools and one of the sessions we are asked to run is deportment, to help students with their posture. I am always surprised that so many youngsters are not encouraged to sit up straight as this portrays confidence, alertness and interest, something vital for job interviews, for example. If I am confronted with rows of sacks of potatoes in a classroom, I take a chair and sit as they are sitting. I then ask them if I look interested in what they are about to say and invariably they answer 'no'. Nobody realizes the negative body language signals they are sending out unless somebody tells them.

Before sitting down, feel the chair with the back of your legs then lower yourself on to the seat and rest your 'seat' at the back of the chair, enabling you to sit straight but feel comfortable. If the chair seat is long but your legs aren't, sit in the middle of the seat. Perching on the edge makes you look anxious. Hands should be loosely clasped or with one resting on top of the other on your lap. Legs or ankles can be crossed, but knees must always be together to make women look elegant, and men should avoid the 'ankle on knee' pose.

## WALK TALL AND LOOK STRAIGHT AHEAD

If you look at the way most people walk, you will notice that it is often with a bowed head and eyes focusing on feet or pavement. Look up! Your field of vision is wide enough to allow you to see any hazards on the ground, so walk with confidence and purpose. Wear a pleasant expression on your face; a broad grin might give the wrong impression, but there is no need to look blank or miserable! Take confident strides – not too long or too short – and place one foot in front of the other in order to stop you swaying like an old-fashioned sailor. Keep shoulders still and arms relaxed. Swing them slightly if that comes naturally to you; you don't want to look like a robot.

On our etiquette courses, we ask everybody to walk with a book on their head, as the old-fashioned finishing schools once did, because this really does promote good deportment. It keeps the shoulders still, the chin parallel to the ground and the eyes looking straight ahead. Walking should look elegant and effortless and, even if you are in a hurry, try not to take huge steps or look as if you are desperate to catch a bus.

Walking tall and with conviction means that you are much less likely to be a victim of crime. Police statistics show that muggers will go for easy targets: if you walk like a victim, you are more likely to become one. Avoid trouble by always looking as though you know where you are going and have a destination in mind.

## Putting it all together

Stand and sit tall. Make the most of your height, whatever it is, by making yourself as tall as you can. This does wonders for your overall posture as well as making you look confident and competent. Walk with purpose, with your chin parallel to the ground. When entering a room, look straight ahead at the people you are meeting, close the door behind you without looking at it and smile! This helps you gain control of the situation immediately and make the most of your personal space. When leaving, walk towards the door and then turn to look at the people you are saying goodbye to. Open and close the door with one hand without showing your back, so that the last thing they see is your face.

The old tip on how to look elegant when getting into a car wearing a dress or skirt is still valid today. Sit on the seat and then swing your legs in, keeping knees and ankles together. When alighting, swing legs out first, knees and ankles together, and push up with the hands to enable you to stand. It may sound rather prissy, but it does take the curse out of showing too much leg, or worse!

As you more than likely have the technology at your fingertips, ask a friend to video your deportment. It is only by seeing the way you stand, sit and walk that you can judge how you come across and whether you are projecting the confident, competent image you want to portray.

# 9 Mind your manners

> *'HIGGINS: The great secret, Eliza, is not having bad manners or good manners or any other particular sort of manners, but having the same manner for all human souls: in short, behaving as if you were in Heaven, where there are no third-class carriages, and one soul is as good as another.'* George Bernard Shaw, *Pygmalion*

> *'There is not a man of common sense who would not choose to be agreeable in company; and yet, strange as it may seem, very few are.'* *The Town and Country Magazine*, vol. 11, 1779

> *'All the important roles shortly boiled down to one: remember you're with other people; show some consideration.'* Lynne Truss

> *'Laws control the lesser man. Right conduct controls the greater.'* Mark Twain

> *'Manners is the key thing. Say, for instance, when you're growing up, you're walking down the street, you've got to tell everybody good morning. Everybody. You can't pass one person.'* Usain Bolt

It is said that good manners can open more doors than a good education. Whether that is true or not, good manners are vital to communicating with confidence. Misunderstandings can often be misinterpreted as bad manners, so it is important to get the communication right. 'Misunderstandings don't exist, only the failure to communicate exists.' So says a Southeast Asian proverb. But what are manners, and do they matter?

Manners and etiquette are different things. Whereas etiquette is the code of rules by which a society lives, manners involve the way people treat each other. Having good manners means behaving in a way that is socially acceptable – in business as well as in private and domestic life. If we all followed the guidelines of good manners and mutual respect, we would treat each other more kindly, behave more honestly and enjoy more professional and social success.

When meeting new people for the first time, it is imperative to use those all-important first few seconds to make a good impression. Smile! Smiling instantly makes you look warm and friendly and puts people at their ease. These days some women take exception when men offer a seat or to open a door – they see it as patronizing. That's a shame, when it puts men off doing what is in fact a simple act of common courtesy.

Good manners are ageless, classless and priceless and everybody should have them. Somebody once said that manners are for the plain, the pretty can get away with anything. It is also the case that the rich sometimes *think* they can get away with anything. This may hold true for a while, but in the end even the richest, best-looking person who constantly behaves in a boorish way will begin to irritate or offend others.

## BEHAVE WITH COURTESY TOWARDS OTHERS

How often have you seen a woman struggling on to a train with a baby in a pushchair, or witnessed people pushing past an elderly man who is trying to manage a heavy case on an escalator with nobody offering to lend a hand? Manners have evolved as our expectations and behaviour alter, but there are still some courtesies that ought to be observed.

Any man should offer to carry a heavy bag or suitcase if he sees someone having difficulty. Giving up a seat on a crowded bus or train to someone not as physically fit as you is also good manners – whether you are male or female. Elderly people and pregnant mothers should always be offered a seat, but don't make a big thing of it. A glance in that person's direction as you start to get up should be enough to let them know your intentions. If he or she is happy standing, just smile and sit down again. If you are that person, either accept appreciatively or decline, thanking the person offering for their thoughtfulness.

In other contexts there are other civilities that are worth observing. For example, in the domestic setting it is polite to stand up when someone enters the room you are in, and so is holding a door open for someone to go through it. These are common courtesies that in this modern age should be adopted by both men and women, as they show regard and consideration for others.

## PRACTISE YOUR HANDSHAKE AND KNOW WHEN TO KISS

The spoken greeting of 'How do you do?' or 'Good morning' (see Secret 3) should be accompanied by a handshake, the quality of which will vastly affect the impression you leave. It is difficult to judge your own handshake, so it is worth practising it with a friend.

The handshake began as a gesture of peace; since most men are right-handed they carried their sword in a scabbard on their left side, so if they extended their right hand, it showed that they held no weapon and therefore came in friendship. The handshake is a gesture of trust and respect, commonly performed on meeting, greeting and parting from another person, as well as when completing an agreement or expressing congratulations.

A good handshake is firm, without crushing the fingers. Nor should there be any excessive pumping or shaking: a firm clasp and one shake is all that is required. Limp, damp or weak handshakes can leave the receiver feeling as though they have shaken hands with a lettuce; not a good way to embark on a new relationship! In the past, a lady would have 'given' her hand to a man. Very grand ladies would have proffered just two or three fingers – and this as recently as the twentieth century. Today, it is acceptable for both men or women to make the first move towards a handshake.

The kissing issue has become more complicated over time, not less. In the last century, people only ever kissed a member of their family in public. In the UK, most of northern Europe and North America, that was just the one kiss. Other European countries have endorsed at least two kisses; Holland doesn't consider itself over-effusive with three, and four is not uncommon in parts of France; it can take ages to go in to a party.

Social cheek kissing has become common, but is fraught with difficulties. Your first decision has to be which side? It can be embarrassing if the two participants head for the same side. If in doubt, stay back and shake hands. It is not good etiquette in Britain to kiss anyone on first meeting them, particularly a man kissing a woman. However, if a man extends his hand, but a woman leans in for a kiss, it would be positively churlish to resist! Of course, there are many cultural differences. Americans tend to be less reserved and more tactile than the British. In Russia, the Middle East and in some European countries, social kissing is common between men, as is embracing.

## RESPECT CUSTOMS THAT PROMOTE GOOD MANNERS

Some customs may seem a little quaint nowadays, but we should consider whether they display good manners – that is, consideration for others – in which case we should take care to preserve and follow them. For example, you might think it old-fashioned when a man settles his partner into a chair before himself sitting down to dinner. However, this is demonstrating care and consideration for someone else.

Should men even now walk on the outside of the pavement when accompanying a woman? This old and quite pleasing custom stems from a time when gentlemen shielded their ladies from getting splattered by slops being thrown out of upstairs windows. Later, it was to stop them being splashed by passing carriages and to protect them from drunken blackguards and thieves. Again, this custom shows consideration for the fact that a crowded sidewalk can still be a hazardous place.

Other examples of good manners are that a man should walk upstairs behind a lady – to be able to catch her should she fall. He should also go downstairs first for the same reason. It is



1 2 3 4 5 6 7 8 9 10 11 12 13 14 15 16 17 18 19 20 21 22 23 24 25 26 27 28 29 30 31 32 33 34 35 36 37 38 39 40 41 42 43 44 45 46 47 48 49 50

likewise good manners for a man to open a car door for a female passenger. This doesn't have to happen every time – many women jump from the car before their escort has had the opportunity to get to their door – but sometimes it is good to give a man a chance to open the door for you, especially on a first date.

## Putting it all together

Some customs dating back hundreds of years are still observed today, even though everybody has forgotten the reasons for them; other traditions still have practical uses today. To many people, manners are unfashionable, out of date and elitist, designed to make people feel uncomfortable if they don't know the conventions, whereas they should guide you seamlessly through most situations with behaviour that will give you the confidence to know how to conduct yourself in any situation, from a society ball in London to a barn dance in Nebraska.

It is difficult, in this age of political correctness and equal opportunities, for a man to know just how he should treat a member of the opposite sex. Not so long ago, men had a definite role in society as breadwinners, while the women stayed at home to look after the household. People knew their place and what was expected of them. Since the roles of men and women have blurred, people have become uncertain about what is correct behaviour, especially towards the opposite sex. However, these social changes should not alter the way we behave towards and respect each other.

The people who come on our courses say that women still like to be treated 'like ladies' when taken out on a date, even by their husbands. In *Everybody's Book of Correct Conduct*, first published in 1893, a man was instructed to guard his wife 'not as a slave, but like a jewel, with care and forethought'. While that might now seem archaic and perhaps patronizing, I can think of a few wives, partners and girlfriends who would like to be treated as a jewel every so often – and so would their men.

# 10 Play the name game

> *'My mother took great relish in introducing me as "This is my son – he's a doctor but not the kind that helps people."'* Randy Pausch

> *'Tell me with whom you associate, and I will tell you who you are.'* Goethe

> *'When women kiss it always reminds one of prize fighters shaking hands.'* H. L. Mencken

> *'The social kiss is an exchange of insincerity between two combatants on the field of social advancement. It places hygiene before affection and condescension before all else.'*
> *London Sunday Correspondent*

> *'You had me at "hello".'* Film: *Jerry Maguire*

Not being introduced properly to someone you want or need to meet, and not knowing how to establish an introduction, can be a nightmare. It is difficult to be a confident communicator if you don't know someone's name, so we need to know how to meet and greet a person properly. Introductions can be awkward, especially if you're not good with names, but you can use various techniques and ploys to help you with this; and you need to find out what works for you.

Try one of the following to help you remember the name of a person to whom you have just been introduced:

1. Repeat it back to the person in the hope that it sticks: 'Nice to meet you, Mr Wood.'



9 10 11 12 13 14 15 16 17 18 19 20 21 22 23 24 25 26 27 28 29 30 31 32 33 34 35 36 37 38 39 40 41 42 43 44 45 46 47 48 49 50

2. Visualize something to do with the name. Mr Wood might be associated somehow with a tree; Ms Wakefield with a meadow of alert cows.
3. Say, 'I'm sorry, I've forgotten your name' and, if the other person replies 'It's Jane', you can say, 'Of course, I know it's Jane, it's your last name I can't recall.'
4. Use a little flattery to gloss over your memory lapse: 'I'm sorry, but I was so riveted by our conversation that I have forgotten your name!' These words, combined with a megawatt smile, should restore your new acquaintance's self-esteem.

The correct etiquette with introductions is for the man to be introduced to a woman, not the other way round. In the past, this would have taken the rather formal, 'Mr Clarke, may I present you to my wife.' While this proves the rule – may I present *you* to *this lady* – there's a more relaxed approach today, such as, 'John, I don't believe you have met my wife. Lydia, this is John Clarke'. This also gives the woman concerned the choice between calling him John or Mr Clarke.

## USE THE CORRECT FORM OF ADDRESS

**At social gatherings, people often prefer to be introduced by their first names, but some don't, so it's best to err on the formal side.**

You may think that titles are something you will never have to bother about, but if you are suddenly asked to introduce a duke and you have no idea what to call him, it can be embarrassing. When introducing a duke, you would say 'His Grace the Duke of So-and-so', and if you are addressing him formally or you happen to work for him, you would say 'Your Grace' or simply 'Duke'. The same applies to a duchess.

A marquis, an earl, a count and a viscount are all introduced as Lord So-and-so – their titles are reserved for envelopes or when describing the person. The same applies to a marchioness, a countess and a viscountess: she is Lady So-and-so; only European counts and countesses are addressed as Count or Countess So-and-so.

Use 'Lord' and 'Lady' in much the same way as you would use Mr and Mrs. A knight of the realm is Sir Jasper, and his wife is Lady Conway. Archbishops and bishops are introduced as 'Archbishop' and 'Bishop', whereas a Cardinal is addressed as 'Your Eminence'.

The royal family has its own protocol, and palace staff usually brief people before they meet the Queen, but if you happened to be introduced to her on a 'walkabout', initially you would address her as 'Your Majesty' and thereafter as 'Ma'am' (pronounced like jam). For the royal Dukes and Princes you would use 'Your Royal Highness' initially and then 'Sir'. Princess Anne, The Princess Royal, is addressed as 'Your Royal Highness' and then 'Ma'am' (again, like jam). An Ambassador or High Commissioner is introduced formally as 'His/Her Excellency' or 'Ambassador'.

## NEVER FORGET A NAME

Plenty of business deals and romantic dates have failed because someone couldn't remember the right name at the right time. Being able to recall someone's name and pronounce it correctly in a face-to-face situation can impress people and set you apart as a confident communicator. Forgetting the name of someone you've met several times can do the opposite.

One effective strategy already mentioned is to repeat the person's name. Do this both in your head and out loud, repeating it as soon as possible after you have been introduced and then occasionally during the conversation: 'How do you do, Sam,' or 'Sam, it seems ages since we last met, it's really good to see you.' Don't overdo it, however, because it can sound ridiculous. Using someone's name two or three times in quick succession –'Hello Diana, how are you Diana? Have you had a good day, Diana?' – is *not* the way to do it, but repeating it now and again is a good way of imprinting a name on your memory and keeping it in the forefront of your mind.

## TRY THE TRUSTED TRIGGERS AND TRICKS

Benjamin Levy, author of *Remember Every Name Every Time*, advocates the FACE method: 'focus, ask, comment and employ':

- **Focus:** concentrate on the person's face.
- **Ask:** find out which version he or she favours – 'Do you prefer Edward or Ed?'
- **Comment:** say something about the name and cross-reference it in your head – 'My uncle always liked Ed, too.'
- **Employ:** put the name to use – 'It's very nice to see you, Ed' – to drive it home.

Try to associate names with things people tell you about themselves: careers, hobbies or holidays, for example. This will help trigger the sound or association of the name in your mind. You can also play the name game of mnemonics: 'Fred works in a shed' or 'Jan with the permatan.' Using alliteration is another way of cementing names: Gail from Guernsey' or 'Alan from Allerdale.'

Never be afraid to ask someone to repeat his or her name. Remember to start out with a compliment: 'I've enjoyed your jokes so much I have totally forgotten your name!' or simply say: 'I'm so sorry, I didn't catch your name.' If you realize that you've forgotten the name a few seconds after being introduced, you will find in most cases that honesty is the best policy.

## Putting it all together

When introducing people, especially if you are the host, it is a good idea to give some snippet of information to provide a springboard to launch a conversation. It is still correct to introduce a man to a woman, a younger person to an older one and junior staff to senior staff in business. For instance, 'Susie Wells, this is Andrew Johnson. He's just moved into the area and likes to play squash. You're a member of the squash club aren't you?' And it is always best to introduce people, even if you find out that they already know each other. If you think that two people might have met but are not sure, then saying, 'Tom, you know Nigel Briggs don't you?' will allow you to introduce them in a way that works whether or not they are already acquainted.

When you are introduced to someone, repeat their name in your response, to help you remember it. It is important when somebody introduces someone as their 'partner' to establish whether it is in a business context or personal relationship, as it can lead to some unfortunate misconceptions!

Once you have been introduced, say 'How do you do?' in a formal context. 'Good morning', 'Good afternoon' or 'Good evening' are also suitable, or even 'Hello' if the situation is less formal. To help you remember new names and drive them into your brain, play some name games like mnemonics or alliteration, and repeat the name as soon as you have been introduced. Being able to remember names is indispensable in the business world and is a great advantage socially too, so find a method that suits you and develop it if you want to became a really confident communicator.

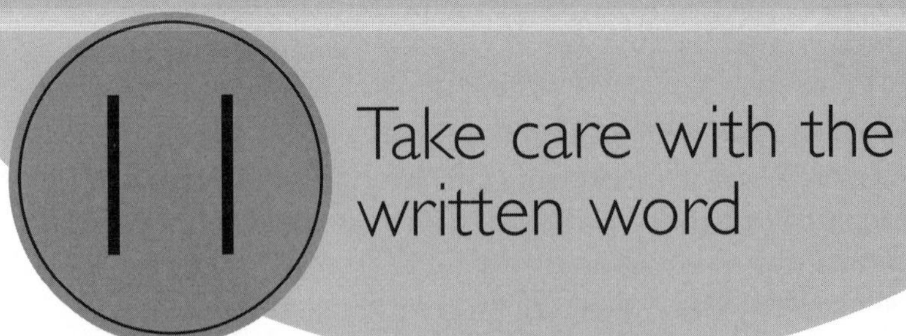

# 11 Take care with the written word

> *'Every writer I know has trouble writing.'* Joseph Heller

> *'How wonderful it is to be able to write someone a letter! To feel like conveying your thoughts to a person, to sit at your desk and pick up a pen, to put your thoughts into words like this is truly marvellous.'* Haruki Murakami, *Norwegian Wood*

> *'And none will hear the postman's knock*
> *Without a quickening of the heart.*
> *For who can bear to feel himself forgotten?'*
> W. H. Auden

> *'The act of putting pen to paper encourages pause for thought, this in turn makes us think more deeply about life, which helps us regain our equilibrium.'* Norbet Platt

> *'Politeness is as much concerned in answering letters within a reasonable time, as it is in returning a bow, immediately.'* Lord Chesterfield

> *'Either write something worth reading or do something worth writing.* Benjamin Franklin

The technological revolution in the twenty-first century has changed the way we write to each other. Many people hardly 'write' letters nowadays; they type an email or text. However, in order to be a confident communicator it is as well that you know the rules for writing a letter. It can make all the difference when writing a covering letter for a job interview – letters that are badly spelled or grammatically incorrect with poor punctuation will not usually get a second glance.

**If you begin 'Dear Jane', then you should sign off 'Yours sincerely, William'. If you know your intended recipient well, you could use 'Best wishes' or 'Kind regards' or even 'Yours'. If you begin 'Dear Mr Smith', you should end with 'Yours sincerely, William Brown'. If you are writing 'Dear Sir' then 'Yours faithfully' is how you sign off.**

For a handwritten letter, *how* you write is also critical. Writing with a good pen is essential if your handwriting is going to look impressive, and don't forget that the fact that we make up our minds very quickly about someone on first appearances also goes for handwriting. Practise developing your own handwriting style and then polish it, but don't let it stint your creativity. Let the writing flow, making sure the characters are even and the lines are straight so that the overall impression is one of sophistication and professionalism.

A fountain pen still has the edge but, if like me, you tend to get ink on your fingers, a good rollerball will do. Good writing paper is also fundamental in projecting the right image. It doesn't have to be as thick for business correspondence as you might want to use socially, but using very flimsy paper can give the impression of parsimoniousness. That doesn't mean that your domestic stationery has to be as thick as parchment, but nice headed paper in cream, white or blue with envelopes to match always looks stylish and should be part of your 'brand', as discussed in Secret 6.

## WRITE COVERING LETTERS AND CVs THAT GET YOU NOTICED

Before you even think about a job interview, you have to make sure that your application gets noticed and is interesting enough to get you the interview in the first place. The covering letter should be targeted for the particular organization, addressed to the person who has invited the application. Here are some key points to take into account when writing a covering letter and a CV:

- Most prospective employers spend an average of six seconds reading a CV, so make sure yours is neat, well organized and to the point.



1 2 3 4 5 6 7 8 9 10 11 12 13 14 15 16 17 18 19 20 21 22 23 24 25 26 27 28 29 30 31 32 33 34 35 36 37 38 39 40 41 42 43 44 45 46 47 48 49 50

- Never use a generic covering letter, as this will put most prospective employers off.
- The CV should not undersell or oversell and, like the covering letter, should be tailored to the needs of the job for which you are applying.
- If there are spelling mistakes, most people will immediately dismiss your application, unless you are the only relevant person for a particular job.
- Only use good white paper if you are sending your application in the post. Email your application only if you are asked to do so.

Use your CV and covering letter to highlight your good points. For example, if you have high-level qualifications, include them; if you only scraped a pass for something, leave out the specific mark. Highlight anything unusual about you that will make you stand out from the crowd: if you have walked from John O'Groats to Land's End, don't just list your hobbies as 'walking.'

If you left school without many qualifications, simply state the years you were in secondary education and then list the courses you have been on since. For example, you might have taken an online course or learned a language. Make another list of the 'transferable skills' you learned in your previous jobs; even something such as organizing the firm's Christmas party will make you attractive to a prospective employer because it shows you have organizational skills. It is not just the fact that you joined the basketball team, but how you contributed.

## WRITE INVITATIONS THAT TELL YOUR GUESTS WHAT THEY NEED TO KNOW

For a big event or party, send your invitations out six weeks in advance. Even though this is a correct amount of notice to give people, it is often best to get the invitation out earlier, especially at busy times of the year. For example, if you are planning a wedding for New Year's Eve, you will need to let everybody know a year in advance so that you – or your guests – can book hotels. You can always mail your friends with a simple 'Save this date' message and then send them the formal invitation later.

Make sure that the invitation states time, place, dress code and the type of occasion (drinks, lunch, dancing, etc.).

**Time** For drinks or cocktail parties, it is advisable to put the times of both arrival and departure on the invitation, especially if you are going on to have dinner, as your guests need to know what time they are expected to leave. Two hours is the correct time for a drinks party. If there is no time stated and you are invited for 7 p.m., you can anticipate the party to be ending at about 9 p.m. At more formal dances, 'Carriages at 2 a.m.' tells your guests when they should be ordering their taxis.

**Dress code** If your invitation states 'Black tie' it means that men should wear a dinner jacket (see Secret 4). 'Informal' simply means wear a smart suit rather than a dinner jacket. (The original meaning was 'no tails and no medals'.) 'Smart casual' means that a blazer, shirt, tie and chinos are safe – guests can remove their jacket and tie if everyone else is more casual. 'Casual' on an invitation can mean anything from jeans to shorts – for something like a BBQ either would be suitable. If you are unsure about dress code, it is fine to check with your host.

The name of the guest should be written by hand on the top left-hand side of the invitation and it is always best to ask for a reply by putting RSVP (*répondez s'il vous plaît*) with your address. This means that you can keep a check on numbers.

## WRITE GREAT THANK-YOU LETTERS

There are two reasons for writing a thank-you letter:

- It's a simple way of showing gratitude to someone who has done something kind for you.
- It keeps open the channel of communication between you, which keeps your name in their mind and helps cement your bonds.

Always write your thank-you letters within one week of an event. They can be written on headed paper or you can choose an appropriate card. The old rule was that you didn't have to thank people for drinks, only telephone after a lunch party, write a note after a dinner party and write a letter covering two sides of the paper after a weekend stay. These days, it is considered polite to thank somebody even if you have been to their house for just drinks, let alone lunch, and certainly for dinners, dances and overnight stays. Letters should also be written to say thank you for gifts and after any unfortunate incident in someone else's house: if you break something or spill red wine over their carpet, an apology in your thank-you letter is a must – preferably accompanied by a bouquet of flowers.

Thank-you notes and letters should be handwritten and, to create a really good impression, written with a fountain pen and black ink. When using a postcard, there is very little space so you don't need to use 'Dear So & So' or end with 'Yours sincerely'; just write the message and end with your name.

## Putting it all together

Be taken seriously and show that you are a confident communicator by making sure that everything you write is well presented and completely correct. This means checking spelling, grammar and punctuation and using good-quality materials; this is part of your 'brand'.

Well-presented CVs should be organized to be easy to read and with a clear typeface on white paper, and take up no more than two sides. They should list your most recent job first and contain something special on the first page, without going into too much detail. Your covering letter should be interesting and attention grabbing (but not flippant), to show your personality.

Invitations should be sent out at least six weeks in advance, and include information about dress code as well as time, place and type of event. For drinks or cocktail parties it is advisable to put times of both arrival and departure on the invitation, especially if you are going on to have dinner, as your guests need to know what time they are expected to leave.

Good manners dictate a swift reply to invitations, preferably within a week. This is all part of giving others the impression that you valued their kindness and helps to enhance their view of you as an excellent communicator.

# 12 Understand netiquette

> *'So in everything, do to others what you would have them do to you, for this sums up the Law and the Prophets.'* The Bible, Matthew 7:12

> *'To err is human. To really foul things up requires a computer.'* Anon.

> *'No matter how well you know the rules of netiquette, you will eventually offend someone who doesn't.'* Don Ritter

> *'Sorry I accidentally cc:ed you in an email insulting you.'* Anon.

> *'You're not obligated to follow/friend anyone. No matter what. Not even your mother.'* Chris Brogan, *An Insider's Guide to Social Media Etiquette*

With email, the intranet and the Internet, don't hide behind your computer. Don't ever email or topline someone with something that you wouldn't say to their face. Not only will you have to live with the consequences of your words, but all computers carry a record of communication, so if someone is affronted enough, they *will* be able to prove what you have said and when. And how many times have you woken to the vague memory of having texted, emailed or posted something that you might not have done had you not had a glass or two of wine?

We all find our own level with email correspondence. To a sibling, parent or friend, you probably just write your missive, add a couple of kisses and hit the send button. However, when you are writing to a stranger for the first time, a more formal structure is needed, similar to standard letters. In this case, 'Dear Mr/Mrs/Ms', with the



9 10 11 12 13 14 15 16 17 18 19 20 21 22 23 24 25 26 27 28 29 30 31 32 33 34 35 36 37 38 39 40 41 42 43 44 45 46 47 48 49 50

sign-off 'Kind regards' or 'Best wishes' would be appropriate. 'Yours sincerely' or 'Yours faithfully' is not generally used in an email. As communication becomes more frequent, first-name terms might be acceptable, with a simple 'Yours' to end the email.

If you're unsure about any of this, simply follow the lead of your correspondent. If he signs off as Peter, then you should write back to Dear Peter. When communication becomes sufficiently laid back as to involve a simple 'Hello' or 'Hi', then you can do that too. Very regular correspondence becomes more conversational, with no address or pay-off: 'Would 3 p.m. be good for you?' 'Sure, 3 p.m. at your office. See you then.'

When sending mail to multiple recipients, it is common practice for some people to type in all the addresses in the 'To' section of the email, but this means that all recipients will be able to see who else has received that message, which might not be appropriate. It is not your remit to give out other people's email addresses without their permission. If you want to keep their emails hidden, use the Bcc (blind carbon) field on the message header.

## FOLLOW THE RULES FOR EMAILING

Following a few simple rules for emailing will help you avoid making errors that could lead to embarrassment – or worse.

1. Always check your spelling and grammar before you send an email. If this is your first contact with a new colleague or client, you need to make the right impression. Not bothering to use a spellcheck, decent grammar or capitalization shows a lack of respect for the person you are contacting as well as for yourself.
2. Always include a subject line. Whether it is a personal or business email, having a concise subject line can save the other person time when searching for your email in a few months' time, or when scanning quickly through emails pending.
3. Have respect for other people's time and bandwidth. Write the message and only add the recipient's name once you have read it. This avoids the possibility of sending it to the wrong person – which can be highly embarrassing, if not downright dangerous.

4. Do put your contact details as a signature on the end of every email. It is most annoying for people to have to trawl through previous correspondence in order to find a phone number.
5. Change the subject title for new subjects. This may sound obvious, but it is surprising how many people return the email with 'Re' whatever the subject was. This is not only lazy but it can mean that you send a raft of emails that could contain derogatory remarks or confidential information.

## AVOID THE DANGERS OF EMAIL

Here is a list of don'ts to bear in mind when using email.

1. Never email in anger – once your email has gone it is nearly impossible to get it back. If you write an email in a state of high emotion or need to send a strongly worded message, don't click send until you feel calm again. Send it straight to the drafts file as soon as it is finished and leave it there for at least half an hour. Once your temper has cooled, read it again and decide whether you still want to send it.
2. Don't write words in capitals because this comes across as aggressive, as if the sender is shouting.
3. For those humorous round robins that brighten anyone's day, never forward the joke with a list of email addresses still plastered all over the header. Consider whether there is real merit in what you are sending and whether the recipient needs to know, wants to know or will enjoy reading it. If the answer is no, don't send it.
4. Don't get annoyed because your text or email is not answered immediately. People are busy, so don't clog up your friends' and colleagues' inboxes with unnecessary trivia.
5. Avoid subject lines such as 'Hello'. This is vague and to a busy person it virtually guarantees that they won't give it much attention – they will consider it to be lightweight and not urgent – even though the body of the message may have some key information.

6. Never send your message in just the subject line, unless you have a very good relationship with the recipient. Examples where you might do this include, 'Ready to go to lunch?' or 'Did you get Jo's message?' Remember that, when an email is open, other people can read the sender and subject lines.
7. Do not forward an email to another person who was not included in the original email without considering the repercussions. Some people don't appreciate their message (with their contact details within it) being passed along, however trivial or innocuous it may seem to you. If in doubt – ask first!

**Furthermore**

Hugs – represented by Os – and kisses – by Xs – are only appropriate in social correspondence. They should be avoided in business, however well you know the person.

## COAX AN ANSWER TO YOUR MESSAGE

When you need an answer to something and you have not received a reply within a reasonable space of time, then send a subtle prompt. It is important not to make the recipient feel intentionally bad mannered, so it might be an idea to blame the email server. Forward the original email you sent and include a note saying, 'So sorry if you already received this last week but my email has been playing up and several people have told me they haven't received my emails, so I am sending this again in case you didn't get it. Hope to hear from you soon.' This should prompt them in to sending a response. If your query is urgent, you will have to resort to speaking to them on the phone.

## Putting it all together

Email is an instant form of communication, but when our inboxes are full to bursting with yet another joke or offer of a Russian bride, it is sometimes hard to sort the wheat from the chaff, so try to send mail that your recipients want or need to receive. Let people know that you have received mail and tell them you will answer fully as soon as you can.

If you are out of the office or away from home, put on an 'out of office' bounce-back responder. Be specific in your message. Instead of writing 'I am away until Thursday', write 'I am away until Thursday 6 June.' Remember to switch it off when you arrive back to avoid confusion and redundant auto-responders being sent out. Thanking by email, rather than writing a letter, is now permissible, as is replying to an invitation if an email address is printed. Socially, you may thank a friend for a lunch or something similar by email if you know them well, although it is always nice to thank them in writing once in a while.

# 13 Maximize the power of phoning and texting

> *'My mind is constantly going. For me to completely relax, I gotta get rid of my cellphone.'* Kenny Chesney

> *'I don't even own a cellphone.'* Jack Nicholson

> *'I love the freedom of movement that my phone gives me. That has definitely transformed my life.'* Richard Branson

> *'Apparently we love our own cellphones but we hate everyone else's.'* Joe Bob Briggs

> *'1 in 10 [survey respondents] said they'd rather lose their mother-in-law than their cellphone.'* Leger Marketing

The mobile phone is now an indispensable part of life for most of us, but it can be a curse as well as a blessing. It is impossible to switch off if you never switch your phone off, but some people would rather their oxygen supply was turned off than their phone. We have all seen examples of people sitting round a table and texting instead of talking to each other. It seems that young people, especially, are losing the ability to read body language because so much of their contact with friends is via text or email. This is having an impact on their ability to get jobs because they are not well versed in basic social skills.

Because our mobile phones are now so central to our lives – most of us would feel as if we had lost a limb were we to lose our phone or have it stolen – we need to develop some etiquette around using them. For example, it is gross ill manners to send bad news by text – for instance to sack someone or end a relationship.

Research suggests that people all over the world now commonly use their mobile phones during business meetings. This is not only disrespectful to other people, but it wastes valuable time and money because meetings start late, run late and are less productive than they should be. If you are trying to buy a concept, product or service from someone and constantly stop to answer the phone, you are likely to lose your train of thought or miss vital information. Unless there is a good reason, phones should be turned off or put on silent during a meeting with anyone.

**To be a confident communicator on the phone, it is important to speak clearly and listen attentively – and to smile. That may sound inane, but a smile really warms the voice and so will help you to give a good impression over the phone.**

## USE YOUR PHONE WISELY AND DON'T LET IT DISTRACT YOU FROM THE IMPORTANT THINGS

The simplest and most important rule is that the people you are with should take priority over the people on the end of the phone. Nothing is more unnerving than to have someone surreptitiously glancing at their mobile while you are trying to talk to them. This really is the height of bad manners because that person is suggesting that the people at the end of the phone are more highly valued than you are.

If someone gives up their precious time to meet you, the least they should expect is your full and undivided attention. You wouldn't try to carry on two verbal conversations at the same time so, for this reason, don't ever text while talking to someone else. You don't want to send the unfortunate signal that the person in your presence is insignificant and uninteresting.

If your phone does ring or a text message arrives, and you realize that you have forgotten to pick the children up from school or you're about to miss a dental appointment, it is acceptable to excuse yourself and phone back or send a text before returning to the conversation. Obviously you should turn off your phone anywhere where you would be mortified if it suddenly leapt into life – such as in the middle of a funeral or a classical concert.

Don't leave your phone continually in view; if a phone is left on a desk at a meeting or on the table in a restaurant (really bad manners – I'm sure you never do it), it immediately sends the message that your thoughts and priorities are elsewhere. The phone is like a magnet: if it is in view, you will keep looking at it.

**Furthermore**

Be careful what you tweet! Systems now monitor Twitter to analyse people's personalities and character traits to use in job interviews. Once you have sent a Tweet it is there permanently, and it can be retrieved by both scrupulous and unscrupulous people.

## KNOW HOW TO ANSWER THE PHONE

The first words you say on the phone are vital: they paint a picture of you if the caller has never met you. How do you come across on the phone? To find out, record yourself and listen. Does the recorded message on your answerphone sound as though you are filled with doom and gloom? If so, record the message again until you sound more cheerful and welcoming.

When answering the phone, it used to be the common custom to state your telephone number, which reassured the caller that they had dialled the right people. Worries about security – and much longer phone numbers – mean that we no longer want to do this, so it is fine just to say 'Hello' and your name. For a business greeting, 'Good morning/afternoon, Mayfair Ltd; how can I help you?' is correct. 'Hey', 'Hiya' or 'Wassup' does not give a professional first impression! 'Hello, William Smith's phone' is suitable if you answer on someone else's behalf.

There is also no reason to answer the phone with a downbeat and grumpy-sounding 'Hello'. Yet again, record and listen to yourself and develop your own telephone style. Starting with just 'Hello' can be a bit abrupt unless said with the intonation that you know who is calling, so help the caller by saying your name.

## KNOW WHEN NOT TO USE YOUR PHONE

So many people miss precious opportunities by answering a mobile instead of talking to the people they are with at the time. I went to a wedding recently where most of the guests spent most of their time on their mobiles. It was true that the photographs did take a long time, but surely the importance of any social event is to talk to and get to know as many people as possible? The very idea of taking a mobile to a wedding (let alone allowing it to go off in church) seems extraordinary. It is far better to leave it locked in the boot of the car or, if you absolutely have to have it on you, turned to silent in a pocket or handbag.

The same is true of parties and networking events. If you don't listen to what is being said with your full attention, you might fail to ask all the right questions, which means that you won't have all the information you need if you want to follow up on a business opportunity. Going out for a meal with friends should be a hugely enjoyable event but, if someone is persistently answering the phone, it spoils the occasion for everyone. There was a time when it was unusual and therefore somewhat thrilling when your date suddenly answered the phone during dinner, but those days have long since gone and now a romantic dinner for two can suddenly become a rather unromantic threesome if the mobile joins you at the table.

## Putting it all together

Today we carry our offices with us and need never be out of touch with anyone at any time. But do we really need to be always at the end of a phone? Much business is done over the breakfast, lunch and dinner table, so if you are constantly answering the phone at the same time you are implying that the person you are with is not as important as whoever happens to call. In my work as an etiquette specialist, I have met quite a number of businesspeople who decide not to sign a deal because of this type of crass behaviour. It does *not* make you look important to be in constant receipt of mobile phone communications during a business meeting. What you are actually saying is that you have no respect for the person whose time you are taking up.

**The people you are with should take priority over everyone else.**

If you have to leave your phone on for a really important call, tell the assembled company and then, when it rings, leave the room or make the conversation as brief and unobtrusive as possible. Don't text while talking to others and don't constantly check for texts; the text is hardly ever so important that it has to be answered immediately. If your call is going to take time, suggest that the others carry on with what they are doing before you leave the room or the table. If you are dining with just one person, be as quick as you possibly can, otherwise they won't know whether to carry on, let their food get cold or just go home.

It is necessary to treat this marvellous invention with thoughtfulness if we are to respect the privacy and feelings of others, as well as keep the work–life balance we all seem to be striving for. We wouldn't be without our phones, but let's use them to enhance rather than rule our lives.

# 14 Use social media with care and attention

*'You are what you share.'* Charles Leadbeater

*'The thing that we are trying to do at Facebook is just help people connect and communicate more efficiently.'*
Mark Zuckerberg

*'LinkedIn is for the people you know. Facebook is for the people you used to know. Twitter is for people you want to know.'* Anon.

*'In the long history of humankind, those who learned to collaborate and improvise most effectively have prevailed.'*
Charles Darwin

**innocent face** Sally Bercow

Social networking is now an everyday part of most of our lives and the way we use it is evolving almost day by day. Social networking is an additional tool for enhancing our professional and social relationships, but it should be used with care. The outburst surrounding old tweets from now ex-youth police commissioner Paris Brown was a reminder that anything you post might be around for ever – and it can certainly come back to haunt you.

The first thing you have to ask yourself is how you want to appear. How often do you want to engage with social media, and what do you want your message to be? Do you want people to think of you as innovative and original, or dependable and steady? Remember, too, that everything



9 10 11 12 13 14 15 16 17 18 19 20 21 22 23 24 25 26 27 28 29 30 31 32 33 34 35 36 37 38 39 40 41 42 43 44 45 46 47 48 49 50

posted on Facebook becomes the property of Facebook and can be accessed indefinitely. Prospective employers are wont to go to your Facebook page when you apply for a job; they want to see whether your personal profile matches up to your CV. It is as well to bear in mind that, with devices like Instagram, images from mobile phones can be uploaded and on the Internet in seconds, so at no time have we been under as much scrutiny as we are today. You really have to think before you act because an imprudent exploit can easily ruin a promising career.

To use social media effectively, you have to be confident in your own identity and know the image you want to project to the world. Those working in financial services, for example, might find jokey tweets a little frivolous; if you're an up-and-coming digital entrepreneur, you might want to stand up and be noticed.

**Use all social media sparingly and only when you have something of interest or import to say. Nothing is worse than having endless absurd or tedious messages flooding your inbox, so don't do to others what you don't like yourself!**

## THINK BEFORE YOU TWEET

Even if you have added a disclaimer to your bio saying that the views are your own, that won't stop people you work with from seeing them and it won't exempt you if you bring your organization into disrepute. Good Twitter etiquette is retweeting and responding appropriately to tweets, in a way that shows that you're a good listener and that you're engaging with the community.

Beware of the following potential pitfalls when using Twitter:

- Remember which account you're using. If you send your own views from a company account, it can be highly damaging and a suing or sacking offence. Once the tweet is posted, the damage will have been done.
- Like Prince Harry, when compromising images of him took to the ether and hit the front pages of the world's press, remember that you cannot rely on your 'friends'

not to make the most of photo opportunities these days, unfortunately.
- Twitter, and the Internet in general, can be especially problematic during trials if jurors tweet or Google information that is not presented to them in court. This could soon become a criminal offence.

## KEEP YOUR LINKEDIN PROFILE UP TO DATE

For a network that people use for business, legitimacy and integrity are vital. Make sure you have an up-to-date, appropriate profile picture. It should be on a neutral background and reflect your business image. Don't use a social picture that could undermine your authority.

There are many LinkedIn forums in which you can post, which can widen your network enormously. However, beware of the following potential pitfalls when using LinkedIn:

- Debating in different professional forums can take up an enormous amount of time, so you have to weigh up the actual value to your business against the amount of time spent on what might be an enjoyable but fruitless exercise. Don't over-post in case people think you've got nothing else to do or have no clients. It can also look as if you're desperately seeking praise and validation from your professional peers.
- Remember to manage your privacy settings. You can now tailor your privacy settings so that new connections don't show on your profile updates. This can be especially significant if you're employed and don't want your boss to know you are job hunting.
- Most importantly, be polite and be aware of your professional image. The virtual world is an extension of the real world and the usual rules of consideration should apply.

## USE FACEBOOK WITH DISCRETION

Facebook is a brilliant way to keep in touch with people and it can be done with minimum effort. A single post carrying news about yourself or your organization can be picked up by thousands of people. However, in this increasingly impersonal age, personal communication in the form of an email or a phone call is becoming increasingly important. But Facebook is a key tool in your toolbox, provided it is used with discretion.

Facebook is a great way to advertise events and experiences and to invite guests to parties, especially those that are going to be held in public spaces like clubs or restaurants. It gives you the option to use a suitable picture to illustrate the invitation. On Facebook there is no space to write the dress code, apart from in the 'event description' box, so make sure you specify it there because people like to know what to wear. It is also a good idea to hide the guest list for your event, so as not to offend those who are not on the list.

The 'may be attending' function can be a minefield, since it is impossible to plan properly for anything if you have no idea how many people are going to attend your event. (If the event is going to be held in a pub or club where you are buying your own refreshments, it is less crucial.) The only time that you should select this option, if you have been invited to a function, is when you are unsure whether you will be in the area or country on the day, or if your plans are likely to change nearer the time. Even then, it is thoughtful to send a private note to the host explaining why. You have been invited because your host wants you there, so try not to disappoint!

## Putting it all together

Social media have transformed the way many people live, socialize and do business. We are more connected than ever before but, as with most things that are broadly beneficial, there are downsides to be aware of:

- Once something is out there on the Internet it stays there and can be accessed by anybody for years to come. Prospective employers, journalists, advertisers and the authorities increasingly use social media to find out more about you, and things that you might have done in the past and since regretted can come back to trouble you.
- It's easy to post something without thinking carefully about the consequences. Never post when you have had a few drinks or in anger, as this is the time you are most likely to get yourself into hot water. You could even find that you have committed a criminal offence.

Think carefully before you Tweet, Instagram or Facebook anything!

Use networks like LinkedIn to further your business. Update your profile regularly with a suitable, current picture of yourself and join forums that are genuinely going to get you more business.

# 15 Shed childhood influences

*'No one ever told me I was pretty when I was a little girl. All little girls should be told they're pretty, even if they aren't.'*
Marilyn Monroe

*'A little thought and a little kindness are often worth more than a great deal of money.'* John Ruskin

*'As a teenager I was so insecure. I was the type of guy that never fitted in because he never dared to choose. I was convinced I had absolutely no talent at all. For nothing. And that thought took away all my ambition too.'* Johnny Depp

*'The world is full of people who have never, since childhood, met an open doorway with an open mind.'* E. B. White

*'I believe in pink. I believe that laughing is the best calorie burner. I believe in kissing, kissing a lot. I believe in being strong when everything seems to be going wrong. I believe that happy girls are the prettiest girls. I believe that tomorrow is another day and I believe in miracles.'* Audrey Hepburn

Childhood experiences can have a huge effect on our lives as adults, but most people have no idea how much negative experiences in childhood can undermine their confidence and their ability to communicate with ease. If you have never been praised as a child, it means that you have probably not got the bedrock of confidence that allows you to make a fool of yourself or 'have a go' at things when you feel uncomfortable.

To shed these negative influences and become a confident communicator, you have to do various things. The first thing is to stop blaming your parents – which many people do – and the next is to stop feeling sorry for yourself – which some people do. Instead, analyse why you think and feel as you do. Going back into your childhood with a dispassionate eye can really help you understand why you feel vulnerable in certain circumstances. Did anyone tell you that you were good at something as a child? Did your parents praise you if you did well at sport, or helped around the house? Did your teachers inspire you to achieve?

**Boosting your self-esteem is vital to becoming a confident communicator.**

It is not just adults who, unwittingly or not, might have eroded your confidence. Jealous siblings or school 'friends' who told you that you looked fat, or that no one liked you because you had spots, were destroying your confidence with every jibe. You cannot change what happened in the past, but you can put it into context and learn from the incidents before eliminating them from your memory as much as possible. You have to learn to ditch your childhood baggage, which isn't easy, especially if you had a bad time at school. Bullying has a lot to do with lack of confidence, and cyber-bullying today is even more toxic because it can reach anyone at any time.

## ANALYSE YOUR PAST EXPERIENCES

When we are young, most of us have very few inhibitions and assume that people will like us. We have not yet learned what is considered 'polite' or 'impolite', so we say what is on our minds and act on impulse. This is forgiven in children but, as we grow older, such behaviour becomes less and less acceptable, and this is often when we are told to 'mind your manners'. The way in which this is done can have a negative impact on your psyche, and this can stay with you for the rest of your life.

It is therefore important that we explain to children *why* they shouldn't say something, rather than just telling them not to be rude, or that the matter doesn't concern them. When children reach the age of eight or nine, they become much more self-aware and telling them off in public can have a lasting detrimental effect.



1 2 3 4 5 6 7 8 9 10 11 12 13 14 15 16 17 18 19 20 21 22 23 24 25 26 27 28 29 30 31 32 33 34 35 36 37 38 39 40 41 42 43 44 45 46 47 48 49 50

**Furthermore**

The old saying, 'Families who eat together stay together' has a ring of truth: meal times should be a time for communication and discussion, whether it is about world affairs or what has happened at school that day. Learning to have your say often starts at the meal table so, if you never had that advantage, it could go some way to explaining why you may lack confidence as an adult.

If you can pinpoint when you first felt anxious about talking to people you don't know, it can help to put everything into perspective. If you were scrutinized by a critical team of teachers when you had to speak at your school, it might have made the experience a nightmare and eroded your confidence. For example, one of my clients was a successful entrepreneur who had been asked by her daughter's school to give an inspirational talk to that year's leavers. She was frantic with fear, so much so that she couldn't go through the school gates without feeling sick. We went through her own school days and she eventually remembered that, as a small girl, she had a squint and had to wear a patch over one eye. All the children avoided or ignored her and every break time she stood alone in the playground feeling invisible; this made her miserable and dejected. She had completely erased this time of her life from her memory, but once she confronted her fears she realized why school held such terrors for her. After analysing her feelings, she was able to get everything in proportion and begin to look forward to giving the talk.

## CHALLENGE YOUR NEGATIVE BELIEFS

Do you think you have nothing to offer when it comes to conversation? Do you feel so insignificant that no one will want to get to know you? Do you imagine that you are not beautiful enough to attract the attention of others? There is nothing like writing down why you feel anxious to help you analyse these, usually false, assumptions. Do you have an open mind when it comes to meeting other people or do you make assumptions and jump to conclusions about people because your parents or peer group at school told you they were not your type or not worth bothering with?

To get rid of childhood influences, you have to challenge those assumptions and beliefs, so write down all the people and situations that have made you feel lacking in confidence and analyse them one by one. Then start thinking for yourself, trusting your own gut feelings and developing a positive frame of mind.

## CONTRIBUTE TO THE CONVERSATION

What are you reading? What films or TV programmes do you like? What are your hobbies? Where do you like to go on holiday? Do you have any pets? All these simple topics will generate a conversation. Asking questions to draw people out and being interested in your environment will also help.

It is also worth remembering that most people are not always happy with themselves or with their appearance, and that virtually everyone feels unsure of themselves from time to time. However, we all have our own unique attributes. Like everyone else, you are an irreplaceable, special person with something important to contribute, but you have to believe that and put things into practice in order to become a confident communicator. That means going to a party or a meeting expecting people to like you because you know you have something to offer. This will generate positive energy and send subconscious signals to others that you are worth talking to.

### Putting it all together

Be aware that many of our negative beliefs and fears start in childhood. Analyse disparaging beliefs and challenge the source of those attitudes so that you can see them for what they are and begin to change them. You have two choices if you want to be a confident communicator: to stay as you are or to move forward; and shedding your childhood influences will help you do just that.

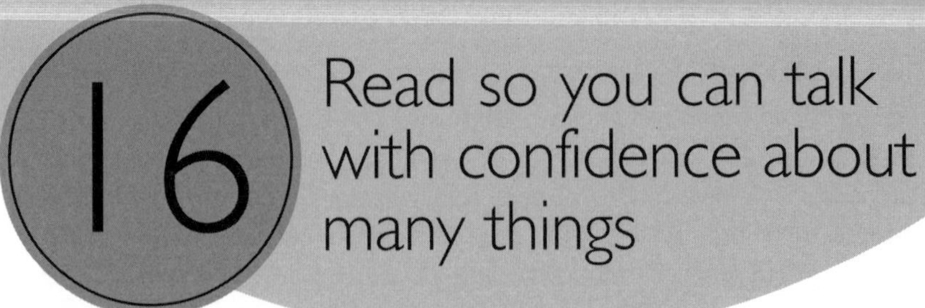

# 16 Read so you can talk with confidence about many things

*'A good book on your shelf is a friend that turns its back on you and remains a friend.'* Anon.

*'The worth of a book is to be measured by what you can carry away from it.'* James Bryce

*'Books let us into their souls and lay open to us the secrets of our own'.* William Hazlitt

*'Always read something that will make you look good if you die in the middle of it.'* P. J. O'Rourke

*'The smallest bookstore still contains more ideas of worth than have been presented in the entire history of television.'* Andrew Ross

Most people in developed countries today can read, but there are disturbing statistics to show that many students leave school with merely basic competence. These statistics are very worrying because, although we live in an increasingly audio-visual society where diagrams are displayed and machines speak, it is still fundamentally important to be able to read and interpret language.

Many of us get most of our news from TV and radio because we find it convenient and we can keep up with the nitty-gritty of world affairs quickly and easily. However, we don't get the added value that comes from reading a newspaper, whether it is a paper or online. We don't get the richness of language or the descriptive words that come from a good writer or journalist and we don't get the diverse points of view that come from reading different journals that enable us to form a balanced view. If you don't read the papers or serious magazines, you miss out on a whole lot of interesting articles and nuggets that never hit the headlines.

It is important to keep up with your partner, your colleagues, your friends and your children and, if you don't bother to read, it is more difficult to do this. If you do nothing else, read the paper every day (especially one of the broadsheets) to keep abreast of current affairs as well as the latest fashion and health tips and to be able to join in discussions regarding business matters. Having a good knowledge of the world is vital for work, getting a job and being a confident communicator. But what if you find reading tedious or even boring? With all the billions of books available, there is bound to be a genre to suit you and the important thing is to *enjoy* what you read.

## KNOW WHAT TO READ TO EXPAND YOUR KNOWLEDGE

While it is essential to get pleasure from what you read, it is important to try to make sure you learn something too. This does not mean reading only features and non-fiction: novels can teach us much about other people and other worlds, as we get to know fictional characters and learn how they deal with their dilemmas and problems. As well as being stories that both entertain and inform, novels need to be well written, with a good, rich vocabulary so that you can expand your word power too.

If you want to be a confident communicator, you should be able to talk about and have a view on a host of different topics. The latest books and issues making the headlines as well as current affairs always provide good subjects for conversation. Celebrity magazines will allow you to keep up with the latest gossip if that is what your friends like to chat about but, if you want to feel confident in any company, it is essential to read something with a little more breadth and depth. Authors such as Shakespeare, Charles Dickens and Jane Austen, for example, not only write brilliant stories that give an insight into life in past centuries but also tell us something about human nature today, as well as reminding us of the many catchphrases coined by such writers that have become part of our language.

Anniversaries bring events back into focus and produce TV and radio programmes and reams of newsprint. The anniversary of the First World War brings the War Poets into the spotlight, and offers an opportunity for studying their work, which will allow you to talk about them. For example, reading Wilfred Owen will give you insight into his opinions of the dreadful conditions he and thousands of young men suffered. Similarly, 2014 is the centenary of Dylan Thomas's birth and reading *Under Milk Wood*, which was written as a radio play, will allow you to talk about how this genius of description wrote.

**Furthermore**

Reading great authors will help expand your vocabulary when you are writing talks and presentations. You will also find that your speech becomes more interesting as you subconsciously use different words to describe what you see and how you feel. All this helps to improve confidence.

## KNOW HOW TO FIND OPPORTUNITIES FOR READING

If you have a very busy lifestyle and if, like me, you tend to fall asleep as soon as you open a book at bedtime, finding the time to read can be tricky. Most people do most of their reading when travelling on trains and planes, before they go to sleep or when on holiday, but wherever or whenever you find the opportunity, just take it and read!

Book clubs are an excellent way of encouraging you to read something you might not otherwise try. The fact that you have to discuss the book also means that you have to finish it. And reading and preparing for a discussion gives you the opportunity to think more carefully about a book in order to form an opinion. It also means that you hear various other opinions about a book. In addition, you can build up a store of books you like and recommend them to others – thus providing another occasion for discussion.

If you find it difficult to pick up a book, there is always the audio version. This means that you can listen while you are at the gym, out running, driving or even working round the house. The only thing about listening rather than reading is that you don't have to use your imagination in the same way and the impact of spelling, grammar and vocabulary is not as strong.

**Furthermore**

It's essential to know the types of book your children are reading because these books can have a profound effect on their psyches as well as on their education.

## KNOW HOW TO READ

With so many tablets and smartphones able to store books, you can easily read almost anywhere and at any time. It is really personal preference as to whether you like the feel of paper between your fingers or whether you enjoy the convenience of technology. Both have their advantages. A book doesn't need a Wi-Fi signal or electricity, but a tablet is ideal for taking on holiday or on a business trip since it can store thousands of books, the weight of which would certainly send you over the baggage allowance limit. If you want a tablet to be your main source of reading, do some research because some have better screens and are easier to use than others. Many magazines and newspapers are also available online and equally accessible while you are on the move.

If you are going to have a discussion about anything – on democracy in the western world, for instance – you would be well advised to read several books on the subject in order to have an even-handed opinion, and the same goes for the life of an icon like Marilyn Monroe. Reading magazines like the *Economist* and *Time* helps you keep abreast of what is happening in the world in a very concise and easily digested form. But whatever you read, it will help you shape your opinions and give you something to say, and this will in turn give you confidence.

Whatever your area of interest – whether it is antiques, chess, arts and crafts, music or sport, for example – there is a specialist publication for you, which will keep you on top of what is happening in your subject.

## Putting it all together

Reading expands the mind, and it means that you can converse with many different people on many different topics, and communicate with more confidence. To communicate well, you have to have enough knowledge to be able to have a valid opinion. It is useful to learn a little about a lot of subjects so that you can talk about most things. Even if, for example, you are not particularly interested in golf, find out who the main players are and even some of their handicaps. Keep up to date with what is going on in the world so that you can discuss politics, finance, art, theatre, climate change or sport and anything else that interests you and that is likely to interest others.

Reading really does open up a whole new world, and having a broader knowledge of that world is what will enable you to communicate with confidence. Nothing is worse than being left out of the conversation or being made to feel ill-informed, but your newfound confidence will also mean that, if you don't know anything about a subject that people are talking about, you will not be afraid to ask questions about it.

Try and make time to read and choose the method that suits you best, be it paper or electronic. Join a book club if you want to try pastures new, as it will help you get other people's points of view. The main thing to remember, when deciding what and how much to read, is that knowledge is power and knowledge gives confidence.

# 17 Take your mouth to the gym to give your voice the edge

> *'Speak clearly, if you speak at all; carve every word before you let it fall.'* Oliver Wendell Holmes

> *'Whatever words we utter should be chosen with care, for people will hear them and be influenced by them for good or ill.'* Buddha

> *'I loved fencing and dancing and elocution.'* Vivien Leigh

> *'My own dreams fortunately came true in this great state. I became Mr Universe; I became a successful businessman. And even though some people say I still speak with a slight accent, I have reached the top of the acting profession.'*
> Arnold Schwarzenegger

> *'I shouldn't be saying this – high treason, really – but I sometimes wonder if Americans aren't fooled by our accent into detecting brilliance that may not really be there.'* Stephen Fry

Your voice is your most important instrument when it comes to confident communication. If you learn to play it well, it will pay dividends. With the technology we have at our fingertips – most mobile phones have a voice recorder app – it is surprising that people still don't listen to themselves and therefore have no idea how they sound. How can you use your voice if you don't know it? Being a confident communicator means knowing how to make the most of your voice.

These days there is no pressure to lose a regional accent, and we value the marvellous mosaic of dialects in the UK and



9 10 11 12 13 14 15 16 17 18 19 20 21 22 23 24 25 26 27 28 29 30 31 32 33 34 35 36 37 38 39 40 41 42 43 44 45 46 47 48 49 50

elsewhere, but clear diction is essential if you are to communicate comfortably. To speak clearly, you have to open your mouth and use the organs of articulation: the tongue and the lips. The tongue is a muscle and needs exercising like any other if you want it to be supple and enable you to speak with clarity.

## LEARN TO SPEAK WITH EXPRESSION

Look at the following sentences carefully and say each line with the feeling the words require. Now record yourself and listen back – does your voice show the emotions in the adjectives?

- It's a *lovely* morning.
- It's a *beautiful* morning.
- It's a *gorgeous* morning.
- It's a *dull* morning.
- It's a *horrible* morning.
- It's an *atrocious* morning.

Read these next lines, stressing *only* the words in italics. This will show you how stressing different words subtly changes the meaning of a sentence. Now record yourself and listen back – can you hear the variation?

- *HOW* many tigers did you see?
- How *MANY* tigers did you see?
- How many *TIGERS* did you see?
- How many tigers *DID* you see?
- How many tigers did *YOU* see?
- How many tigers did you *SEE*?

Now do the same with these lines:

- *I* packed the sandwiches.
- I *packed* the sandwiches.
- I packed *the* sandwiches.
- I packed the *sandwiches*.

Practise these lines:

*Jonathon Jo had a mouth like an O*
*And a wheelbarrow full of surprises.*
*If you wanted a bat*
*Or something like that*
*He had it, whatever the size is.*

## TRY SOME TONGUE TWISTERS

There is nothing like tongue twisters for limbering up the mouth and the brain. The following sentences will not only oblige you to use the tongue, lips and teeth, but they will also make you read what you see and not what you *think* you see, helping to keep the brain agile too.

The consonants are really important letters because they 'punctuate' the sentences. 'T's and 'D's are almost extinct in some regions, but if words just fade away they are hard to understand. It is a sad fact that a large number of people will have lost a significant amount of hearing by the time they reach their late thirties. The growing use of iPods and mobile phones, as well as loud music at concerts and in clubs, means that ears are damaged, and they don't repair. If you have experienced your ears singing for days after a concert, it won't have done a lot for your hearing.

Record yourself repeating these tongue twisters, paying special attention to the consonants. Then listen back.

1 Six sick hicks nick six slick bricks with picks and sticks.

2 I wish to wish the wish you wish to wish,
But if you wish the wish the witch wishes,
I won't wish the wish you wish to wish.

3 Stupid superstition! (Say three times)

4 There was a fisherman named Fisher
Who fished for some fish in a fissure.
Till a fish with a grin,
Pulled the fisherman in.
Now they're fishing the fissure for Fisher.

5 To sit in solemn silence in a dull, dark dock,
In a pestilential prison, with a life-long lock,
Awaiting the sensation of a short, sharp shock,
From a cheap and chippy chopper on a big black block!
To sit in solemn silence in a pestilential prison,
And awaiting the sensation
From a cheap and chippy chopper on a big black block!

(by W. S. Gilbert of Gilbert and Sullivan from *The Mikado*)

6 If Stu chews shoes, should Stu choose the shoes he chews?

7 Luke Luck likes lakes.
Luke's duck likes lakes.
Luke Luck licks lakes.
Luck's duck licks lakes.
Duck takes licks in lakes Luke Luck likes.
Luke Luck takes licks in lakes duck likes.

(from Dr. Seuss' *Fox in Socks*)

8 Seventy-seven benevolent elephants. (Say three times)

9 I scream, you scream, we all scream for ice cream!

10 Wayne went to Wales to watch walruses.

11 Peggy Babcock, Babcock Peggy. (Say three times)

12 In Hertford, Hereford and Hampshire, hurricanes hardly ever happen.

13 One-one was a race horse.
Two-two was one too.
One-one won one race.
Two-two won one too.

14 Celibate celebrant, celibate celebrant, celibate celebrant, …

15 Willy's real rear wheel. (Say three times)

16 Six sleek swans swam swiftly southwards.
Swan swam over the sea
Swim swan swim
Swan swam back again
Well swum swan.

17 When you write copy, you have the right to copyright the copy you write.

18 Theophilus Thistle, the successful thistle sifter, in sifting a sieve full of unsifted thistles, thrust three thousand thistles through the thick of his thumb.

19 Hassock hassock, black spotted hassock.
Black spot on a black back of a black spotted hassock.

20 How many cookies could a good cook cook
If a good cook could cook cookies?
A good cook could cook as many cookies,
As a good cook who could cook cookies.

21 How much ground would a groundhog hog,
If a groundhog could hog ground?
A groundhog would hog all the ground he could hog,
If a groundhog could hog ground.

## DO BREATHING EXERCISES TO IMPROVE YOUR VOICE

Breathing correctly is essential for good voice control and production. Here is an exercise to help you.

1. Place your fingertips together on your diaphragm (the dome-shaped muscle below your ribs), take a deep breath in and expand the ribcage outwards and upwards, increasing the size of the chest. Then breathe out. Your fingers should come apart as you breathe in and meet again as you breathe out.
2. Breathe in again (keeping your fingertips where they are) and hold the breath for a count of five. Breathe out to a count of five, but this time hum as you expel the air. Keep your mouth closed so that you can hear the sound resonate in your head as you expel the air.
3. Breathe in to a count of five and then say 'aah' as you expel the air with your mouth open.

Repeat the exercise on your own until you can increase your breath control to be able to hum and say 'aah' comfortably up to a count of ten.

Then try it again but making the humming and then the 'aahs' softer, then louder. Bear in mind your deportment (see Secret 8) as it affects the way you breathe and therefore the way you speak. To keep your mouth in good trim, practise opening it as wide as you can. Do this ten times in the morning to keep your face and mouth supple.

1 2 3 4 5 6 7 8 9 10 11 12 13 14 15 16 17 18 19 20 21 22 23 24 25 26 27 28 29 30 31 32 33 34 35 36 37 38 39 40 41 42 43 44 45 46 47 48 49 50

## Putting it all together

By listening to your voice, you can understand how it sounds. It is vitally important, when developing your brand and improving the way you come across to others, that you find out how fast you speak, how clearly you speak and whether your voice is interesting. This is the first step in learning to use your voice effectively. Few people have any idea how they sound and those who do often discover that they do not like the sound of their own voices – so listen and analyse what you need to learn.

The way you use your voice is vital if you want to make a confident impression. Good diction is fundamental in being easily understood. Pausing can also be pivotal in helping people to comprehend what you are saying. Accents can cause bias, especially if they are very strong; but they shouldn't be a problem unless they are difficult for anyone outside the region to understand. The most important thing is to be understood, wherever you are, and that means speaking clearly and audibly.

# 18 Put on an act to make a show of confidence

*'Life's like a play; it's not the length but the excellence of the acting that matters.'* Seneca

*'Men acquire a particular quality by constantly acting in a particular way.'* Aristotle

*'Acting is a nice childish profession – pretending you're someone else and, at the same time, selling yourself.'* Katharine Hepburn

*'Life's like a movie, write your own ending. Keep believing, keep pretending.'* Jim Henson

*'I liked pretending to be other people: I could reinvent myself, reinvent my own reality.'* Helena Bonham Carter

Sometimes you need to fool yourself in order to fool others. By this I mean that you have to put on a show of confidence so that others will believe in you. For most things in life you do not need to be an actor, but there are some occasions when it can help to 'think yourself' into a part. This is especially helpful in interviews, when making speeches or when you are very nervous and unsure of yourself. One of the things I found most useful from my time at drama school was learning how to do just that.

There are many different ways of getting into character. One of my colleagues always starts with the shoes. When she is learning a new part and getting to know the character, she researches the shoes that person would wear and then gets some. Once



9 10 11 12 13 14 15 16 17 18 19 20 21 22 23 24 25 26 27 28 29 30 31 32 33 34 35 36 37 38 39 40 41 42 43 44 45 46 47 48 49 50

she is standing in that person's shoes, she literally starts to build the character from the feet up. As an actor, you have to have belief in yourself. Many actors may be shy and insecure, but they all have the confidence that they can play a part with conviction and communicate through that character to their audience, whether on stage or through the medium of TV and film.

## FOOL YOURSELF INTO BELIEVING YOU CAN SUCCEED

If you are really worried about a situation, especially if it is likely to be confrontational, then fooling yourself into believing you can succeed, whatever the circumstances, will give you the confidence to follow through. If you are about to play in a big match, thinking and acting like a winner can really help you achieve success. If you have an oral exam or a presentation to make, acting as though you are full of confidence will fool your brain into believing you *are* confident.

The self-help guru Paul McKenna was working with a golfer who constantly hit his ball into a bunker. He would hit the precise spot every time and Paul realized that he was actually hitting his target, but not the right target; this was because the man had been constantly telling himself to avoid the bunker and the message his brain was receiving was 'Hit that bunker at all costs!' Paul told the golfer to aim for the bunker rather than the green. The man was surprised, but did as he was told – and the ball landed less than a metre from the hole.

We all need to act a part at some time and using some professional methods can really help. Drama techniques are not all about pretending to be a tree or a giraffe (although children learn these things) but about thinking yourself into another persona. This can help you distance yourself from problems and fears or give you the confidence to face your demons. If you use a role model as an example, imagine how this person would conquer anxiety and self-doubt. Put yourself in their shoes and imagine how they might react in certain situations. Would they use bravado to bluff their way out of a problem or might they sit down and carefully consider all the options before taking any action? Either way, you can fool yourself to success.

## PUT YOURSELF IN SOMEONE ELSE'S SHOES

It might be useful to try this exercise. The secret in making this exercise work is really to *believe* you are another person.

Go into a quiet space and find a mirror to place in front of you. Now close your eyes. Visualize a situation where you live on the streets and that you are lonely and afraid. It is cold and you are hungry. Reflect on the impact this is having on your life. What are your fears? Do you have any hopes for a future? You might have health problems; if so, would that show in your posture? Most homeless people eventually withdraw from life and this shows in closed, foetal body language. People hug themselves to keep warm and to keep safe, as a means of locking out the world.

Now you must create the back-story for your character. What is your name and what led you to live like this? Why haven't you been able to do anything about it? The causes could be many. You might have been a gambler and lost your job, your home and your family. You might be hooked on drink or drugs, or perhaps you lost loved ones or couldn't cope with the stresses and strains of modern life and had nobody to talk to. You might have been in the armed forces and seen atrocities that will never leave your memory.

It may take ten minutes or it may take an hour, but to fool yourself into believing you are that person, you need to immerse yourself in the character you have created. Where you lived before and what your life was like are questions you need to invent answers to. Were you married, do you have children and where are they now? Do you see any way of getting out of the morass you are in?

Once you feel you are that person, open your eyes and look at your facial expression and your posture. Do you look confident and could you communicate well in this state?

## IMAGINE YOURSELF MAKING IT

Using the methods just mentioned, sit or stand in front of a mirror, close your eyes and visualize yourself as a superstar. How would that star handle the situation you find yourself in? If you are worried about making a speech, imagine how an expert would do it. If you are anxious about going to a party or a networking event, envisage a situation where everyone is waiting for you to arrive and can't wait to meet you.

It may sound trite, but if you walk into the room with confidence and a smile, you will immediately attract people to you and they will want to talk to you.

### Putting it all together

We all have to act a part at some time in our lives. You have to put on a brave face in front of others when you are feeling sad or when something awful has happened. Sometimes you have to act as though you are confident even when you are not, but the more you act the part, the more it becomes reality. Convicted prisoners can lie to themselves so totally that it can be hard for the police to break their story since they genuinely believe what they are saying is true. The brain has the power to convince us and therefore others that we can do something, if we truly believe we can.

Try employing drama techniques to step into another person's shoes. This will help you create a confident character for yourself when you need to. You can use a role model to help you build confidence. Think of yourself as a superstar, imagining how a star stands, walks and sits. Do they smile? Do they make eye contact with people as they pass? Think about how you will behave when you are a winner. For actors, 'Doctor Theatre' will come to your aid, because getting into a character so completely that you believe you are that person will banish sickness, migraines and even croaky voices for the time you are on stage.

If you really have confidence in yourself and act as if you know what you are doing, you will be able to do it.

# 19 Use the power of a positive attitude

> *'Optimism is the faith that leads to achievement. Nothing can be done without hope and confidence.'* Helen Keller

> *'If you have no confidence in self, you are twice defeated in the race of life.'* Marcus Garvey

> *'Delete the negative; accentuate the positive!'* Donna Karan

> *'Where men of judgment creep and feel their way, the positive pronounce without dismay.'* William Cowper

> *'Once you replace negative thoughts with positive ones, you'll start having positive results.'* Willie Nelson

A positive attitude is what confident communicators have in common. If you are confident in yourself, you will come across as confident to others. Developing a powerfully positive attitude is not always easy, however: it takes time and it often means making a change in your mindset. Again, a lot depends on your childhood influences, how you are used to being spoken to, in what way you speak to yourself, and how you view the world.

If you have had a number of setbacks in your life and are used to being surrounded by pessimism and negativity, it is difficult to think positively. So what can you do to change your attitude? The first thing is to look again at all the constructive things you have done, the good things in your life and what you have to offer. If you go back into your past experience, you will be able

9 10 11 12 13 14 15 16 17 18 19 20 21 22 23 24 25 26 27 28 29 30 31 32 33 34 35 36 37 38 39 40 41 42 43 44 45 46 47 48 49 50

to identify what has shaped you and given you skills. Write down your list, as in the following examples:

- Dealing with cantankerous, ageing relatives gave me the ability to cope with people who are hard to please; now that I work in the service sector I use this knowledge to deal with difficult customers.
- Holiday jobs and work experience gave me important skills and knowledge about working with different types of people and about how organizations work.

These examples may sound trivial, but they show that *everybody* has something to offer. If you are IT literate, able to cook, sew or drive, if you can speak a foreign language, spell correctly and are numerate, you have important skills. Make a list of your own attributes and abilities: writing them down can help you see clearly what your strengths are, which will help to build up your confidence and create a more positive self-image.

Academic qualifications are not always necessarily as important as we think – ask Harvard dropout Bill Gates. For many jobs, the employer is looking for something other than academic achievement, so think of what qualities you have that will make you stand out from the rest. This need not be any great feat like running a marathon or climbing Mount Everest, but the fact that you can type 80 words a minute, even though the job might not actually require that particular skill, may sway a decision in your favour.

## SWITCH ON THE POWER

We all lack confidence from time to time. Even the most self-assured-looking men and women probably shake in their shoes at the thought of giving a big presentation or facing an important sales meeting or interview. We all feel unsure of ourselves and of our ability at some point. However, if this makes you have negative thoughts to the extent that you think you are going to fail, you are much more likely to do so; if you anticipate a disaster, there probably will be one.

To increase positive feelings, try envisaging the best outcome from a challenging situation you are facing. Strive to make yourself look forward to the situation, whatever it is, and visualize success beforehand. This covers everything, even a confrontation with your children. If you expect to have a problem sending them off to school or getting them to sleep, then you will. If you expect these things to be straightforward, they are much more likely to be. This positive attitude might seem naively optimistic in some situations but, if you aim for a positive focus to your life, this attitude will eventually become second nature and make even the most difficult situations less daunting. Facing your demons makes you powerful. Overcoming and coping with the worst things life can throw at you makes you powerful – so switch on the power!

## RAMP UP THE POWER

Getting to know and acknowledge your weak points is important, because unless you know them you cannot eliminate them. Whatever you feel unsure about must be faced. In some circumstances issues are better avoided or at least delayed until you feel comfortable that you can handle them. If something is very stressful and you know you are not going to be able to cope, don't do it until you feel you can – it is important not to set yourself up for failure.

If you dislike face-to-face confrontation, write a letter or a memo instead, so that you can say what you mean without feeling you are going to lose control of the situation. Give yourself the time and the environment to think clearly and put your point across. If you find that negotiating is a weak point, write down the outcome you are looking for and stick to it. If it is a price, for instance, and you are worried that you are going to be beaten down, the conversation might go something like this:

'Well, Mr Blake, having researched the situation fully, I feel this is the right price for all concerned. To come down any further would mean a lessening of both quality and service, which would be to no one's advantage.'

Have the confidence to follow your own judgement. Both positivity and negativity are communicable and pass from person to person. Try to absorb the positive and disregard the negative.

We are all very good at condemning ourselves, and wondering whether we have the right to expect success. However, if we work hard to achieve our goals, we have every right to expect success.

## SHARE THE POWER

Try to be as supportive as possible of your partner, your children, your colleagues and your friends, because then they will be supportive of you. This will increase your self-confidence and your positivity. Above all, praise others as much as possible! So often, we give people silent compliments such as thinking 'That's a nice dress' or 'He looks really well' so why not say them out loud? While compliments shouldn't be too personal, it gives anyone a warm glow to be told they look well or attractive. A positive attitude generates positive and powerful energy.

**Furthermore**

On some of our courses we do an exercise using metal divining rods, when we ask the class to think first negative and then positive thoughts. When the students are thinking negative thoughts, the tutor can get within a metre or so of the group before the energy they generate makes rods cross, but when they are all thinking positive thoughts the energy field is so wide that the rods will cross when the tutor is at least three metres from the group. We are all made of energy, so make sure the energy you produce is positive.

## Putting it all together

Focus on your good points. You can help build confidence by making a list of your strengths, your talents, your skills and your achievements. These achievements can be in any field, either domestic or at work.

Remember that everybody has abilities and accomplishments to be proud of. Think about yours and focus and concentrate on them.

Compliment others whenever possible, on appearance as well as results. Motivate your staff or colleagues by encouraging new ideas. At work, criticize constructively, pointing out where things have gone wrong and giving guidance on how to improve them – and do it in private if feasible. At home, praise your partner and your children and never take anything for granted. People only know you love them if you tell them so.

Actually visualizing success is helpful in any situation. If you anticipate a problem with your annual appraisal, then you are likely to have one. If you think you will lose an argument with your partner, you more than likely will. If you expect to have a problem getting your children off to school, you will!

An American guru described people as 'radiators' and 'drains' – those who radiate energy and those who drain it. So think positive and you will communicate that positivity with confidence and always be a 'radiator'!

1 2 3 4 5 6 7 8 9 10 11 12 13 14 15 16 17 18 19 20 21 22 23 24 25 26 27 28 29 30 31 32 33 34 35 36 37 38 39 40 41 42 43 44 45 46 47 48 49 50

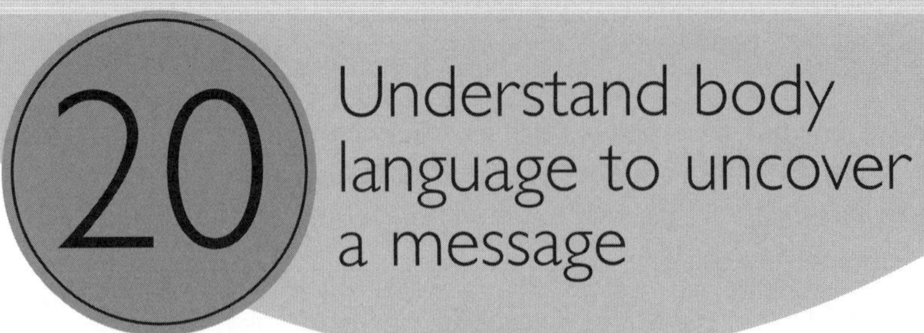

# 20 Understand body language to uncover a message

*'I speak two languages, Body and English.'* Mae West

*'When the eyes say one thing, and the tongue another, a practised man relies on the language of the first.'* Ralph Waldo Emerson

*'ARIEL: 'But without my voice, how can I…*
*URSULA: 'You'll have your looks, your pretty face. And don't underestimate the importance of body language, ha!'*
The Little Mermaid

*'He speaketh not; and yet there lies a conversation in his eyes.'* Henry Wadsworth Longfellow, 'The Hanging of the Crane'

*'As the tongue speaketh to the ear so the gesture speaketh to the eye.'* King James I

Our body talks all the time: we send out conscious and unconscious gestures. Body talk is what the body says: the shaking head, the shrugging shoulders, tapping feet, wringing hands and shifting eyes all send out distinctive signals which are read and interpreted on different levels.

As mentioned before, people usually make up 90 per cent of their mind about us within the first few seconds of the first meeting; and some research has shown that it can be as little as one-hundredth of a second. You therefore don't have much time to make sure that you are projecting the right image and that your body is talking positively. The way you dress or speak, the gestures you use, the way you walk, the way you eat – all this body language helps people to build a picture of you – good or bad.

Positive body talk is vital for confident communication. Positive gestures are part of this and so is appropriate touching. While we have to be careful not to invade someone's personal space, a brief squeeze of the hand or a touch on the arm can do a lot to reassure, comfort or cajole. People who are tactile in this way are often more popular than those who never touch others: using the language of touch enables us both voluntarily and involuntarily to get closer to each other.

Negative body talk causes us get into 'fight or flight' mode, when we are deciding whether to fight the foe or make a quick getaway. At this point we might remain rooted to the spot, sending out distress signals through our body language. In social and business situations things are usually not so dire, but the genetic response from our ancestors is still the same. If you are worried, nervous, angry or bored, you may send out these signals without realizing.

Personal chemistry matters enormously in your dealings with people. We are naturally attracted to people similar to ourselves; it's a bit like an animal recognizing friend or foe by the colour of their fur and the smell of their skin. Your body language plays a huge part in the way you form relationships on a professional and a social level, so make sure you know what your body is saying.

## MAKE SURE YOUR BODY LANGUAGE SENDS THE RIGHT SIGNAL

We send out a number of involuntary signals that tell others whether we are feeling confident or not:

- Fidgeting with the hands, rubbing the nose or eyes or 'washing' the hands slowly shows that you are not at ease with yourself. Hand washing can denote lying, anxiety or insincerity.
- Excessive stroking of the cheek or chin can show that you are reluctant to say what is on your mind, as the body is subconsciously trying to keep the words in your mouth.
- Clenched fists, shifty eye contact and foot tapping can express nervousness, worry, apprehension or concern, and too much crossing of arms and legs can also denote nervousness or unease.



1 2 3 4 5 6 7 8 9 10 11 12 13 14 15 16 17 18 19 20 21 22 23 24 25 26 27 28 29 30 31 32 33 34 35 36 37 38 39 40 41 42 43 44 45 46 47 48 49 50

- Crossing the arms over the chest can be interpreted as a 'barrier' position so, even if it is your most comfortable stance, it is best avoided in professional situations.
- Shrugging of the shoulders also shows frustration or anxiety as the physiological changes in the body send an acid to the muscles, ready for the 'fight or flight' scenario.
- A businessperson infuriated by someone who is late for an appointment will show disapproval by sitting very straight, as will a school teacher or a boss about to reprimand an insubordinate pupil or employee.

Cultural nuances play a part in our interpretation of body language. In the western world, for example, if you constantly look away or over the person's shoulder when talking to someone, they are likely to think that you are bored and want to talk to someone else, or that you do not like them. By contrast, in other parts of the world it is not considered polite to maintain eye contact for too long.

## NOTICE POSITIVE BODY TALK

To become a really confident communicator, get to know the talk your body is talking. You cannot manufacture positive body language without it having the opposite effect to the one intended, and you will be giving an impression of insincerity. Positive body talk comes from within: it comes from being confident and having integrity. It happens unconsciously and shows itself in different ways.

Let's look at some of the positive signals and messages that people send unconsciously, so that you can look out for them in business and social contexts:

- A hand resting on the cheek usually means evaluation or analysis.
- A hand *slowly* stroking the chin often signals consideration.
- Steepling of the fingers shows that the person is listening, helping to build rapport; it also displays confidence.
- Rubbing the hands together quickly shows anticipation and excitement.
- Pressing the hands together usually indicates someone trying to persuade somebody to their point of view.

- Leaning forward with direct eye contact denotes active listening and indicates honesty and interest.
- A quick lifting of the eyebrows means someone is glad to see you.
- Holding the head up exhibits confidence and integrity.
- A genuine smile shows a sincere greeting.

## NOTICE THE BODY TALK OF ANTICIPATION

You might scoff at the idea that people's body talk is so transparent that, if you know what to look for, you can see what people are thinking about, but look around the next time you are at a party or attending a meeting.

Male signs of anticipation, whether of a date or an important meeting, include adjusting clothes, straightening the tie and smoothing the hair. Feet can also show the direction a man's thoughts are taking: if he is attracted or curious, one or both feet will be pointed in the direction of his interest, even if the rest of his body isn't. Women anticipating a date or a meeting tend to play with their hair, sit up very straight and lick their lips. Both sexes will play with objects when getting to know one another. It can be fascinating to watch couples having dinner, for instance. Either sex can find themselves doing something rather Freudian with the stem of a wine glass or an unwary pepper mill! Watch, too, how people will unconsciously push their glass backwards and forwards as the course of the conversation changes, and the attraction ebbs and flows.

## Putting it all together

For body language to give a positive impression, it is vital that the heart, mind and body are in agreement when you speak. If what you say contradicts what you are feeling or thinking, your body language will still give you away to anyone who has read even a little on the subject. Sometimes people are quite unaware of how much their bodies are betraying them, and sometimes mannerisms can become entrenched habits unless someone points them out.

Take the time to notice other people's body language, and see whether you can spot occasions when their body language is in conflict with what they are saying.

When we talk, we may use our hands to emphasize points, but when someone is lying they tend to clasp their hands together or push them deep into their pockets so that they can't give them away with restless gestures. An untruthful person may also cross both their arms and legs at the same time. An indication that the hands are disagreeing with the mouth is evident when the palms face upwards in what is known as the 'hand-shrug'. If somebody is unsure of their facts, they will often use this gesture.

Of course, arm and leg crossing also indicates that someone is in a hurry or wants the conversation to end, or that they are simply trying to increase their energy levels because they are tired. If you really want to know someone's thoughts and build rapport, eye contact is vital because the eyes really are 'the window to the soul'.

# Find out how to be a confident speaker

> *'Patience, persistence and perspiration make an unbeatable combination for success.'* Napoleon Hill

> *'Do not accustom yourselves to use big words for little matters.'* Samuel Johnson

> *'He suffered occasionally from a rush of words to the head.'* Viscount Samuel

> *'Originality consists in thinking for yourself, and not in thinking unlike other people.'* J. Fitzjames Stephen

> *'If I make a fool of myself, who cares? I'm not frightened by anyone's perception of me.'* Angelina Jolie

Most people have to make a speech at some time in their lives, and to speak well you have to be a confident communicator. A good speaker is someone who can inform, inspire and entertain an audience. Good speakers are good because they *want* to make the speech and deliver it in a way that will reach the hearts and minds of the people they are talking to. The best speakers are 'performers' who feel passionate about their subject. You don't have to be an actor to perform well, you just have to believe in your message, believe in yourself and develop your own unique style, which should fit you like a second skin.

No one is asked to talk if they don't have something important to say so, if you are invited to speak, it is because your information will be relevant to your audience. Good speakers



9 10 11 12 13 14 15 16 17 18 19 20 21 22 23 24 25 26 27 28 29 30 31 32 33 34 35 36 37 38 39 40 41 42 43 44 45 46 47 48 49 50

are good because they enjoy grasping the opportunity to deliver knowledge that will help others and they are not afraid of what other people think of them. Very few people want to change places with you when you are giving a speech, so have confidence in the fact that the audience want you to succeed. Nothing is more satisfying; but the message has to be delivered with enthusiasm and confidence because, if it is presented in a lacklustre, unconvincing style, it will not hit home.

Good speakers are both motivating and inspirational because they *believe* in what they are saying. If you don't have faith in what you are saying, why should anyone else? They take the time and trouble to research and prepare thoroughly. Preparation is the key to confidence and confidence is the key to success. Good speakers look 'outside the box' when it comes to giving added value to the topic they are delivering. But one of the reasons why good speakers are good is because they know how to use their voice – see Secret 17.

## RESEARCH YOUR TOPIC THOROUGHLY

There are some essential rules for giving a speech: you have to know your subject, you must be sincere and you have got to be enthusiastic. It is vital to research not only your subject but also your audience because every audience is different and some people will have more knowledge of your topic than others. You have to know how much they know, what else they need to know and how you can make what you tell them motivating and relevant.

**Before preparing a speech, the questions you need to ask are: Why me? Who is the audience? Where am I speaking? How long should my speech be?**

When researching, it is critical to know what you want the talk to achieve. Do you want to inform, influence, recommend a course of action, motivate or entertain? All talks must be interesting and therefore 'entertaining', otherwise your listeners will switch off, which will be a waste of their time and yours, so when you research your material, try to find some anecdotes or analogies to illustrate your points or some 'fascinating facts' that are not generally known. For example, if you were giving a talk about the history of the handshake, a fascinating fact might be that men used to clasp each other's hand to show that it did not conceal a weapon. Interesting anecdotes and inspirational sayings are also a good way to begin and end a speech.

## REHEARSE, REHEARSE, REHEARSE

The common anxieties about making a speech – fear of making a fool of yourself, forgetting what you are going to say, blushing or losing your voice – are all caused by one thing: lack of preparation. Having written your speech, practise delivering it, not once but many times. Being well prepared means honing your speech – so that you have ironed out any mistakes in the content – and practising your delivery so that it goes without a hitch on the day. Feeling well prepared reduces nerves by making you feel confident that the speech you have prepared is the best it can be.

Decide whether you will write out the whole speech to read, or make notes or bullet points to use. If you have access to an autocue or speech prompter, this makes life easier. There is more about this in Secret 28, 'Get a grip on visual aids to make your "show and tell" a success'.

The ideal way to rehearse is to record yourself reading your speech aloud, because it is only by hearing what you plan to say that you can be sure that you are:

- conveying the message you want to convey
- giving the information in a logical, chronological fashion
- speaking clearly and at the right pace
- not repeating yourself
- not using the same 'pet' words and phrases over and over again.

It is a good idea to record the talk first for its content and, when you are sure that's right, to record it again to check your delivery. Only by listening to yourself can you make certain that your message achieves your aims and is clear and to the point.

You don't need to learn a presentation word for word, but the better you know it, the more confident you will be. Some people like to put their bullet points on cards or use notes, or even read out the whole thing, but in each case it is important to know it well so that you can keep contact with your audience.

As stated in previous secrets, believing that you *can* do it is the key to success.

## DELIVER YOUR SPEECH

If you have prepared thoroughly, you will have put a huge amount of effort into researching, writing and rehearsing your presentation. You will feel satisfaction from knowing what you need to say and wanting to say it, and you should now be looking forward to imparting the information, so it would be a shame if your delivery let you down. Not everyone is a natural speaker, however, so don't beat yourself up about it. Instead, follow a few simple rules and tips, as follows:

1. Unless you are giving a very informal talk, stand up. If you are standing, the members of the audience have to look up to you, and psychologically that gives you an advantage.
2. Before you start, wait for the audience to become quiet, take your time and look around the room – and smile! Stopping for a moment before you start helps you calm your nerves and assess your audience.
3. Start speaking slightly more slowly and with a deeper voice than usual, as nerves can make you speed up and become high-pitched. It is not just what you say but also the way you say it that makes people retain the message.
4. Always inject some energy into your delivery, no matter how tired you are or how many times you have given the talk. If you are not feeling positive about your subject, why should anyone else be?
5. Emphasize points as you go along, and be enthusiastic – it comes through in your voice.
6. Look at the audience all the time and try to paint pictures with words.

7. When you answer questions, your presentation is not over; you are still 'under the spotlight'. If the final question is a negative one, make sure you finish with a positive point.

**Furthermore**

The seven important 'Ps' for making a speech are: pace, pitch, phrasing, projection, pausing, posture and practice – which really do make perfect! When speaking in public, speak clearly and a bit more loudly than you would normally. Don't hurry, but vary your pace and pitch as much as possible. Pausing every so often is vital as it can help emphasize a point. It is also a great way to hold the attention of your audience. Don't make your pauses too long, though, since this can sound as though you have forgotten what you were saying.

## Putting it all together

Remember the four vital elements of any presentation: energy, enthusiasm, effort and enjoyment.

To be a good speaker, you have to want to do it. You have to look forward to inspiring and motivating your audience with passion and panache. To achieve this mindset, it helps to be thoroughly prepared. When you rehearse the speech, change the pace and pitch of your voice and listen to how you sound. Listening to and getting to know your voice is fundamental to your success as a presenter, so read your talk out loud and record it. Craft the phrasing of the sentences to make sure they are not too short or too long. Practise the pauses and learn to project your voice so that it fills the room.

Good posture is vital if you are to project confidence as well as your voice, so breathe deeply, stand tall and look the world in the eye. It can be very helpful to rehearse your speech in front of a mirror as well as recording it with a video camera, because this will help you see whether you need to change any annoying habits or develop a more relaxed and confident style.

Most speakers get nervous before making a speech, but you have to control the nerves, so take a deep breath and count to three, then hold the breath for the count of three and exhale to the count of three. This will help slow your heart rate, and calm you down so that you can get your thoughts in order.

# 22 Learn how to make a riveting speech

> *'Everything is practice.'* Pelé

> *'We all have the ability. The difference is how we use it.'* Stevie Wonder

> *'I am always doing things I can't do – that's how I get to do them.'* Pablo Picasso

> *'Sincerity – if you fake that you've got it made.'* George Burns

> *'A man who uses a great many words to express his meaning is like a bad marksman who instead of aiming a single stone at an object takes up a handful and throws at it in hopes he may hit.'* Samuel Johnson

A good speech is one that keeps the audience's attention and delivers the right message. It has to be well researched, well written and well rehearsed as well as informative, entertaining and relevant. It should also tell a story and have a beginning, a middle and an end. Good speeches are good because they are written from experience and from the heart. They don't have to be funny, but they should contain plenty of descriptions so that you are painting pictures with words. Always include some examples and several anecdotes, which add colour to what can otherwise be a dry narrative.

The English language is so rich and varied that you don't have to repeat descriptive words; there are plenty to choose from. Only repeat words for emphasis: 'It is important to remember and it is important to be aware…' Otherwise, you can say: 'It is important to remember and it is essential to be aware…'

Preparing any sort of presentation takes hours, not minutes. Having found out why you are speaking and to whom, put yourself in their seats. Try to answer the questions those people want answered and you will get your points across. If you are addressing a group where you know there are specific concerns, address those issues straight away as people will not settle down and listen properly until their fears are allayed. I have worked with people from all walks of life and helped them write speeches that will connect with their particular audience. But connecting is not enough; speeches, to be good, have to be a performance (see Secret 21, 'Find out how to be a confident speaker'). So, when you are writing your speech, make sure you include words and phrases that will set your audience on fire, or at least attract their interest! Here is an illustration:

'The seminar went very well and everyone enjoyed it. The presentations were particularly informative and instructive.'

Or you could write this:

'The seminar was a great success and the feedback from the audience greatly exceeded our expectations. The speakers were experts in their field and delivered their presentations with passion and panache!'

## ASK THE RIGHT QUESTIONS

You may be asked to make a speech for any number of reasons: you might be a good raconteur, an expert in a particular field, or the best man at a friend's wedding. Whatever the reason, you need to find out the answers to the following questions before you start to write your presentation:

- What size is the audience and what age are they?
- What are their job categories or positions?
- Is it a mixed audience?
- What do they want or need to hear?
- What is the venue like? Its ambience, size and location all need to be taken into account.

If what you say isn't relevant, the audience won't bother to listen, so get as much information as you can from the organizers, whether they are clients, customers or people from your own company or department. Once you know what you need to talk about, the next question is how to make your speech as inspiring as possible. For example, if you make water pipes, you may not think that is the most exciting subject, but just think of what those water pipes are used for: if your pipes are taking precious water across the bush to two hundred villages in Africa, tell that story, paint the pictures and make your listeners see the way the water will transform the lives of the villagers.

Useful phrases like 'For those of us who aren't quite sure…', 'As I am sure you all know…', 'Although we are all aware of…' and 'I think some points may need re-emphasizing…' allow you to include information that some of the audience may already know when others might not.

## ESTABLISH THE LENGTH, CONTENT AND STRUCTURE OF YOUR SPEECH

A speech should only last as long as the information will allow, so don't be persuaded to speak for an hour if your message will only take you 20 minutes to deliver. A good way to gauge the length is by the BBC newsreading speed, three words a second. Write out the speech in full; this may sound cumbersome but it enables you to ensure that it is the right length for the time allowed and that you have included all relevant information and presented it in a logical and easily assimilated way. Don't make the sentences too long: remember that you are writing the speech to be 'said' rather than read.

Keep the introduction short, as its purpose is to grab the attention. A quotation or a fascinating fact is a good way of getting people to listen to you. Use phrases, sayings, examples, anecdotes or analogies to illustrate a point.

**The greatest motivations for anyone to listen to you are fear, benefit and topicality. If you can put yourself between your audience and adversity or save them time, hassle or money, they will listen to you. Topicality is a good hook to make the issue pertinent.**

If you are good at telling jokes, then by all means include some, but bear in mind the journalists' golden rule: 'If in doubt, leave it out.' This also applies to any information you're unsure about. To make sure the speech is succinct and to the point, try condensing your message into a single line and work outwards from there.

A good way to start is to write down everything that could be relevant and of interest. You will need to make several key points and back up each one with evidence before establishing a brief but logical link to the next key point. The aim is to lift your audience's interest with each point. For a short presentation, keep to three or four clearly defined facts. Each point should tell the audience something they need or want to know. It is critical to involve your audience with lots of 'we' and 'us'.

The conclusion is very important. Summarize the major points and make sure the audience knows when you have finished. If you constantly say 'And finally' or 'To summarize', the audience will switch off. Don't end with an apology; make sure the conclusion finishes the talk on a positive note.

## PAINT PICTURES WITH YOUR WORDS

It is said that a picture is worth a thousand words but words can be used to paint pictures too. Phrases, sayings, anecdotes or analogies that you can use to illustrate a point are worth their weight in gold. To help people visualize things immediately, say, for example, 'It's as high as the Eiffel Tower' rather than simply 325 metres or 'as heavy as bag of sugar' instead of 2.5 kg.

Visual aids are also there to help the audience understand the message. Text, graphs, charts and diagrams can be used to explain complex information using programs such as PowerPoint. However, they should not be used as a prompt for the speaker, who should never read directly from the screen, as this is one of the quickest ways to alienate your audience. With all visual aids, you need to be clear about what your message is before you prepare them. Simplicity is the secret: a good guideline for a PowerPoint presentation is to have only six lines of text per slide and six words per line. There is more on this in Secret 28, 'Get a grip on visual aids to make your "show and tell" a success'.

## Putting it all together

When writing a speech, you have to know your subject and you must be sincere. You should be convinced that your message is worth while and that your audience will benefit in some way. Be sure your aim is fulfilled, whether it is to impress, inform or convince, and look at the subject from every angle to make it grab the audience's attention. The questions to ask once you have agreed to make the speech are: Why me?, What is the subject? and What part will it play in the event? It is also useful to know whether there will be any other speakers.

You need to define your audience as accurately as possible and know their requirements. When you have written the speech, ask yourself the following questions about it:

- Is my introduction interesting enough to seize the audience's attention?
- Have I linked each key point with the one before so that everything is clear and logical?
- Is the information in my PowerPoint slides or other visual aids going to help the audience understand the message more clearly?
- Is the conclusion strong and positive?

For a short presentation, keep to at most four clearly defined points or subjects. Each point should tell the audience something they need or want to know. Having made a key point, back it up with sufficient detail to prove it. When taking questions, make sure that you end on an optimistic note. Above all, it is essential to be enthusiastic about your subject; this will help you portray an air of self-confidence.

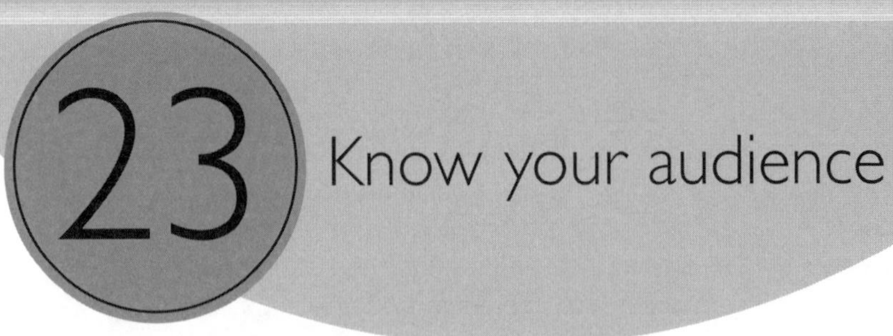

# 23 Know your audience

*'All the world's a stage and most of us are desperately unrehearsed.'* Sean O'Casey

*'Personality is the glitter that sends your little gleam across the footlights and the orchestra pit into that big black space where the audience is.'* Mae West

*'Be impeccable with your word. Speak with integrity. Say only what you mean. Avoid using the word to speak against yourself or to gossip about others. Use the power of your word in the direction of truth and love.'* Miguel Angel Ruiz

*'Your purpose is to make your audience see what you saw, hear what you heard, feel what you felt. Relevant detail, couched in concrete, colorful language, is the best way to recreate the incident as it happened and to picture it for the audience.'* Dale Carnegie

*'I am a real ham. I love an audience. I work better with an audience. I am dead, in fact, without one.'* Lucille Ball

If you are to become a confident communicator, knowing your audience is vital, but how do you define 'audience'? Your audience can be one person or a thousand people or any number in between. The word 'audience' means different things: spectators, addressees, listeners, viewers. It can also describe an interview, a meeting or a consultation. Let's look at these in detail:

- A spectator is someone who watches what is happening but does not take an active part.

- Addressees are receivers of information.
- Listeners describe a radio audience and viewers a television audience (see Secrets 39 and 40).
- An interview audience will probably comprise up to four people.
- A meeting could have any number and a consultation might be with just one person.

Each of these categories requires a different type of knowledge and therefore a different kind of presentation. The important point for any audience is that your message is targeted to them. It may sound obvious but too many people concentrate on themselves rather than the people they are talking to.

The audience will react differently in different situations, so your message has to be written and delivered in different ways. You would not impart the same information in the same way if you were on a stage with an audience of two hundred as you would to three people sitting round a table. The material might be the same but the delivery wouldn't. You might need a lectern and a microphone for a large audience and you would need to project your voice and use larger gestures, but you are unlikely to need these if you are talking to a small group. Weddings and parties are discussed in more detail later, but the essential thing with all types of audience is to do your research and get to know the kind of people you are going to address.

## RECOGNIZE AND IDENTIFY DIFFERENT AUDIENCES

The secret of effective public speaking is to recognize and identify the audience you are going to speak to. Failure to do this is one of the key reasons why speakers fail. The only way to know this is by asking the same questions as when you were asked to speak; why me, who am I speaking to and how long should my speech be?

This is crucial because your message must be relevant and of benefit to your audience. Not only is it imperative to know your subject and be able to talk with sincerity and enthusiasm, but your delivery must be tailored to the audience in front of you if it is not to fall on deaf ears. If your audience is older, you can make your anecdotes speak to their sensibilities, and you can go at a slower pace with more pauses, whereas for a young audience, the sentences would need to be shorter and the pace faster to keep them engaged.

The audience needs to know they are in safe hands and are not going to be bored out of their wits or embarrassed when you stand up to speak. They need to be sure of your objective, whether it is to inform, influence, recommend a course of action, motivate or entertain. If your message is unclear, the audience will eventually switch off.

**Remember the greatest incentives for anyone to listen to you: fear, benefit and topicality.**

## ADAPT YOUR CONTENT TO YOUR AUDIENCE

Here are some examples of audiences you might be asked to speak to. You may have to make a speech at a wedding, a birthday celebration, a hen or stag party, or a corporate event. You could have to address a fundraising or charity committee, a political party, a medical conference, a school or university, your local church or management and departmental meetings at work. Some of the people in the audience might not have English as their first language, which can be an added complication. You may be conveying the same content when you are speaking, but it will have to be delivered in different ways.

Let's look at some examples:

- If you are a politician talking to a party conference, you will have to speak in more general terms than if you were speaking to a small group of constituents, who will expect you to concentrate on local issues affecting them.
- If you are a doctor speaking at a medical convention, your content and approach will vary enormously from the way you would talk to a patient. That is likely to be a one-on-one meeting where you would be sitting rather than standing and you would have direct eye contact – rather than scanning the hall in a large venue.

## BUILD RAPPORT WITH YOUR AUDIENCE

Building rapport with your audience and developing empathy are crucial for confident communication. It all comes down to the content of your talk and how much you can involve the audience. If you have done your research and you know that a large proportion of the audience know more about the subject than others, it can pose a dilemma: how much detail can you go into without turning that part of the audience off?

One useful way of showing that you are aware that some people will know more than others about what you are going to say is to include phrases like:

- 'Many of you will be familiar with what I am about to say, but I think it bears repeating…'
- 'For those of us who aren't quite sure…'
- 'Forgive me if I am going over old ground…'

These types of phrases address these audience members directly and also tell them that others are not as au fait with the topic as they are. I once went on a trade mission with a group of experienced 'missioners' and one or two novices like me. The newly appointed High Commissioner, in his welcome speech, went into great detail about the country we were visiting and I could see the old-timers smothering their yawns and, when he had finished, there were more than a few derogatory remarks. As it was my first visit, I found it very useful, but to have satisfied the entire audience, all the High Commissioner had to say was 'I am sure many of you know more about this country than I do, but I know you will excuse me for going into specifics for the new missioners among us.' It was a classic case of not doing enough research into the audience he was addressing.

## Putting it all together

The 'audience' is the only thing that matters when you are communicating with anyone. It is not what you want to say but what they want or need to hear that is important. This goes for a meeting as much as a speech (there will be more on this in Secret 34, 'Make your meetings productive'). You may not be able to tell your audience everything they *want* to hear; if you are a weather forecaster, people will want to hear that the sun will shine tomorrow but, if it is going to rain, that is what you have to tell them!

Build a relationship with your audience as soon as you can. You do this by making your talk as interesting and as relevant as possible to that particular audience. Speak with integrity and clarity, not just about the information you are imparting but also in the way you speak. Smile at your audience, make them feel at home, invite them to trust you and what you are going to tell them by speaking with an air of confidence and competence. As highlighted before, research is of paramount importance if you are to communicate effectively, so that you know who they are, where they are and why you are talking to them.

# 24 Know your venue

> *'We shape our buildings; thereafter they shape us.'*
> Winston Churchill

> *'If you really want something, you can figure out how to make it happen.'* Cher

> *'Good buildings are designed by good people, and all problems are solved by good design.'* Stephen Gardiner

> *'Some venues are better run than others. Sometimes it's just maddening to deal with full dinners being served in front of your face. You can have a good or bad show anywhere.'*
> Todd Barry

> *'I never played coffee shops; I just played a lot of coffee shop-sized venues. I took every venue I could get my hands on.'*
> Sara Bareilles

Knowing your venue is as crucial to communicating confidently as anything else, whether you are making a speech, giving a performance, throwing a party or getting married. If the venue is too big, you might not be able to reach all your audience; if it is too cramped, people will not feel comfortable and won't be able to see or hear you properly. So, first of all, determine how many people will be there. The next issue is capacity: how big does your venue have to be? Some of the places you might use include a church, a community hall, a restaurant, a dance hall, a private house, a marquee or a barn. You could also elect to hold your event on a beach, in a garden, on a ship, in a shop or at a theatre.



9 10 11 12 13 14 15 16 17 18 19 20 21 22 23 24 25 26 27 28 29 30 31 32 33 34 35 36 37 38 39 40 41 42 43 44 45 46 47 48 49 50

If you want to make your venue really memorable, then by all means think outside the box but still be aware of the practicalities. Is it accessible, is it easy to find, is there plenty of parking? These are just some of the questions you have to ask yourself. As with everything else, research is crucial. It is as well to try and see the venue beforehand, if it is feasible. The more comfortable you are with the venue, the more confident you will be.

**The right location can make or break an event. If people get cold, they will go home early. If the bar is small and they have to wait for their drinks, they might not remember the occasion with much affection. This would be a great pity when you consider the time, effort and money that go into any event.**

## CHOOSE THE VENUE TO MATCH THE OCCASION

It can be hard to choose the right venue, as there are so many to choose from. Obviously the number of people will dictate the size, but there are countless other things to consider. Looking at the guest list or audience breakdown, you have to identify the age group first of all. This is vital because, if there will be a number of older people or young children, lifts, accessible loos and stairs have to be taken into account. If, for example, you are co-ordinating a conference for volunteers for an organization like Help The Aged, the audience is likely to contain quite a number of senior citizens, so the sound system has to be very clear, the lighting bright and the hall itself on the ground floor. If people have to queue for lifts, it can play havoc with timings.

If you are having a birthday party in the garden or on a beach, you will have to consider the possibility of rain in many regions and make alternative arrangements available. Gazebos are useful for protecting people from the odd shower, but what if there is a downpour? Can everyone fit into the house? If you are making a speech outside, wind, birdsong or traffic noise could affect the way you are heard, so a microphone is usually a must unless it is a very small party.

If you are making your speech in a restaurant or dance hall, or in a church at a wedding or a funeral, there will normally be a microphone but, to be confident when delivering your speech, make sure you have a rehearsal beforehand. Community halls or private houses don't often have a problem with heating, lighting or sound, but it is important to create the ambience you want to make your party go with a swing. If you choose to have a party in your house, remove breakables and valuable objects, to prevent them being damaged.

Marquees are popular for a summer event and a number of ships offer interesting spaces for parties or corporate events. If you have to make a speech, you will need to be able to get all the audience in one place so, again, researching the venue beforehand is imperative. If you are using a theatre as a venue, you will have lights and good acoustics built in but, if your speakers are not used to projecting their voices, it is as well to check that there are microphones available; again, a trial run is essential.

## THINK ABOUT THE CAPACITY AND LAYOUT OF THE VENUE

The capacity of a venue is sometimes difficult to gauge. For a party it is better to pack them in, as people relax more if they feel they are part of a crowd. Lighting is also key: soft lights make most of us feel more at ease. However, if the room is too crowded and noisy, people get tired of shouting after a while and they will drift away. This is especially the case with older people; if they are to communicate well, they need more space and more light so, if you are having a family party that includes elderly relatives, don't make the group too large. You will also need to have chairs on hand for some of them to sit down during the evening.

If you are using several rooms in your chosen venue, be aware that the gathering will split into groups and can therefore become disjointed, with some people hardly seeing each other at all. (There is advice on this in Secret 26, 'Know the value of preparation – as host and guest'.) If your company is opening a new shop and you have to organize a celebrity to launch it, it is vital that as many people as possible can see him or her. It is just not the same hearing a disembodied voice from behind a pillar so, if possible, provide a stage or put the star on the stairs, if there are any. If you are lucky enough to have a megastar, make sure that people are not going to cause a traffic jam if they spill out on to the street.



1 2 3 4 5 6 7 8 9 10 11 12 13 14 15 16 17 18 19 20 21 22 23 24 25 26 27 28 29 30 31 32 33 34 35 36 37 38 39 40 41 42 43 44 45 46 47 48 49 50

## BE PREPARED FOR POTENTIAL HAZARDS AT YOUR OUTDOOR VENUE

If your party is on a beach, in a marquee or in the garden, there can be a several potential problems. High-heeled shoes and chairs may sink into sand or wet grass, so provide walkways as well as hard standing for tables and chairs if possible. A marquee can be a very cold place if the weather is bad and, if it is windy, you have the added problem of flapping canvas or plastic, which can make guests uncomfortable and conversation difficult. Be prepared for this by organizing people to tie it down and make heaters available if necessary.

In a barn or marquee the electricity supply can fail and heaters can run out of fuel, so make certain that lanterns and spare fuel are available. Pathways and car parks will need to be lit, not only to stop people tripping and breaking their ankles (not a good start or end to the evening, especially if they decide to sue!) but also to avoid mud or manure in the fields. Allergies from straw or dust in barns have to be taken into account when deciding on your venue, as it is difficult to be a confident communicator if you are sneezing every few minutes. A raised stage should have a step for speakers to use. This sounds obvious, but try getting on to a high stage in a tight skirt!

**Putting it all together**

Choose the venue with your guests or audience in mind, taking care to remember the practicalities. As the whole idea of any gathering is to help people get to know each other and communicate as easily as possible, ensure that there is enough space, adequate lighting and easy access to the amenities as well as food and drink, if you are serving any. Good heaters are essential, whatever time of year you use a marquee or an outside venue in Britain. But even if your marquee blows down in the night and your portable toilets overflow, keep your head, don't panic and look for a solution because there always is one. Even if you have to change the venue at the last minute, there is always something that can be done. Hang on in there and never give up!

# 25 Get to know your event

*'Great minds discuss ideas; average minds discuss events; small minds discuss people.'* Eleanor Roosevelt

*'A positive attitude causes a chain reaction of positive thoughts, events and outcomes. It is a catalyst and it sparks extraordinary results.'* Wade Boggs

*'Where much is expected from an individual, he may rise to the level of events and make the dream come true.'* Elbert Hubbard

*'Winners make a habit of manufacturing their own positive expectations in advance of the event.'* Brian Tracy

*'If you believe that feeling bad or worrying long enough will change a past or future event, then you are residing on another planet with a different reality system.'* William James

Just as you need to spend time on research and preparation in order to get to know your audience and your venue, it is equally important to spend time and energy in getting to know every aspect of the event itself. To be able to communicate with confidence, you need to have a thorough knowledge of the occasion and what it entails or represents, and a firm belief that it will reflect your sense of integrity and high standards.

If you are going to be running the event yourself, you will need to know how to go about it and what you need to put in place. Although every event is different and will have to



9 10 11 12 13 14 15 16 17 18 19 20 21 22 23 24 25 26 27 28 29 30 31 32 33 34 35 36 37 38 39 40 41 42 43 44 45 46 47 48 49 50

be dealt with differently, the planning of any big event will demand a large amount of preparation – whether it is for a birthday, a wedding, an anniversary party or a corporate event. This secret will give you the knowledge you need to run an event that will enhance your ability to be a confident communicator at all types of occasion: parties, formal dinners, conferences, job interviews, meetings, team building and networking events.

The advice on venues in Secret 24 is also applicable here. Proper time must be set aside to choose a suitable venue, and this must be done well ahead – this can mean weeks or months ahead rather than days. Big exhibitions, charity balls and other major events can take up to a year to arrange – often with a huge amount of money at stake. It can be an extremely pressurized experience, so don't underestimate the amount of stress involved. The key to success is thorough preparation and planning: if you are unprepared for anything, you will not be able to connect with people fully because a part of your mind will be thinking 'Have I remembered to tell…' or 'Did I ask…'

**Remember: 'Preparation is the key to confidence and confidence is the key to success!'**

## GO THROUGH YOUR ESSENTIAL CHECKLIST

These are the ten essential steps to take when planning any type of event:

1. Establish the type of event.
2. Agree on the number of people.
3. Pick the venue.
4. Decide on the catering.
5. Choose the decor.
6. Select the dress code.
7. Check the lighting and sound equipment.
8. Choose the type of music.
9. Make a decision on the drinks.
10. Send out the invitations.

**Furthermore**

If you need a band, a DJ, photographers, videographers, make-up artists, extra waiters, bar staff or flowers for the tables and the venue, make sure you organize them in plenty of time because good people in these fields are often booked up for months ahead.

## PLAN THE THEME AND THE CATERING

### The theme

If you are organizing a conference or networking event, the size of the hall and the amenities are what you need to get right. When you invite your delegates or advertise the event, think about the maximum you can manage. It is also worth remembering that the dropout rate can be as much as a third, so you don't want a huge auditorium that looks a third empty. It is always better to have the venue full to capacity, so choose a room that that can be split if you find the numbers fall.

When planning parties, the first things to be decided upon are the number of people you will invite and the theme. By 'theme' we mean dress code as well as decor. If you choose fancy dress, be aware that some people are uncomfortable about dressing up; however, if you are set upon this, a good compromise is to think about 'hats' as a theme or a character from a favourite film or book. Something like this doesn't involve people having to spend too much time or money on an outfit. Make sure the dress code is on the invitation. (There is more information on this in Secrets 4–7.)

As for the decor, this includes ambience, which in turn includes music, lighting and other aspects of the surroundings. Make sure that your decorations are neither potentially hazardous nor flammable, especially if you are going to use candles. Music can make or break an event, too, and needs careful consideration. If it is too loud, people can't talk, so it is often a good idea to confine loud music to just one room. Ensure that the venue is neither too warm nor too cold. Obviously it depends on the time of year and the weather, but a good rule of thumb is to have rooms at a temperature of at least 22 °C when people arrive; the heating can be turned down as the room fills up.

### The catering

Food is crucial at many events, so when drawing up your menu be aware of allergies and food intolerances and steer clear of nuts and seafood. If you are unsure of your guests' religious beliefs, don't serve pork or beef (lamb, chicken and fish are a safe bet) and always have a vegetarian option. If guests have to stand up to eat, the type of food is crucial: it is almost impossible to feel comfortable eating food that requires a knife and fork when standing or perching on a sofa, so avoid large pieces of meat or salad in these circumstances as they are difficult to cope with.

**If you are a guest at a formal event, don't sit down at the table until everybody else does in case a grace is going to be said, and at the end of a meal make sure you leave something in your glass in case there is a toast.**

At a conference or networking event when you are providing light refreshments rather than a meal, it is a false economy to serve inferior biscuits, tea and coffee, so make sure they are fresh and of good quality and, again, serve either finger food or cuisine that can be eaten with just a fork.

See also Secret 26, 'Know the value of preparation – as host and guest.

## GET YOUR SEATING PLAN RIGHT

Formal dinners need a lot of organization if they are to be successful. For a formal dinner for more than ten people, a seating plan and place cards are a good idea, and for a large event you might also need posters of the table plan to show guests where they are sitting, as this will save time and confusion.

Once you know how many people are coming, one of the most important things you have to decide is who is sitting next to whom. This goes for both business and important social meals.

The seating plan is perhaps the most time-consuming thing to arrange, but giving the plan the consideration it needs will be rewarding in terms of the success of the event.

## Putting it all together

If you go to an event with every prospect of enjoying it, the chances are you will. It is just a matter of having confidence in the fact that you have done your research and prepared thoroughly, so there will be no nasty surprises.

If you are responsible for the arrangements, give yourself as much time as possible to prepare. If you leave things until the last minute, you will panic and not be able to think clearly. Give yourself a timeline and stick to it.

- Use the checklist above before you start and look at it again when you think you have everything in place.
- Make sure you communicate properly with all your suppliers and keep a physical record of all transactions.
- If possible, have a back-up plan in case anything goes wrong: for example, by recording an evening's music on your iPod in case the DJ doesn't turn up.

Thus, to be a confident communicator, invite the right people, do your research, plan ahead and the event should be a huge success.

1 2 3 4 5 6 7 8 9 10 11 12 13 14 15 16 17 18 19 20 21 22 23 24 25 26 27 28 29 30 31 32 33 34 35 36 37 38 39 40 41 42 43 44 45 46 47 48 49 50

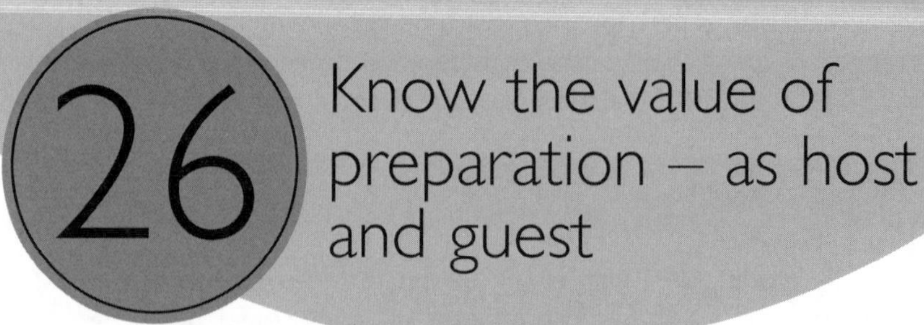

# 26 Know the value of preparation – as host and guest

*'After all, what is your host's purpose in having a party? Surely not for you to enjoy yourself; if that were their sole purpose, they'd have simply sent champagne and women over to your place by taxi.'* P. J. O'Rourke

*'Cocktail party: A gathering held to enable forty people to talk about themselves at the same time. The man who remains after the liquor is gone is the host.'* Fred Allen

*'A host is like a general: calamities often reveal his genius.'* Horace

*'A good host is someone who really takes care of everyone, from the food to their daily programme. I can't.'* Christian Louboutin

*If you would have guests be merry with your cheer, Be so yourself, or so at least appear.'* Benjamin Franklin

For your social or business event to go well, you need to be able to communicate with confidence, and to do this you have to have everything already in place – as we have seen, preparation is the key to confidence. As a host, it is obviously up to you to make sure that as everyone arrives they are introduced to each other and that everyone has enough to eat and drink, depending on the occasion.

Knowing how to be a good guest is just as important as being a good host, but people often underestimate their importance as a guest. You have been asked because your hosts want you there, so not to turn up is extremely rude. It upsets the numbers and possibly also the seating plan if there is one. If your hosts have struggled long and hard to get just the right people together and you let them down, they won't thank you for it. If you know you can't make an engagement, give people as much warning as you can so that your place can be filled, and never cancel for a better invitation – your sins will always find you out!

The most important thing about answering invitations is to do it quickly. Whether it is a small dinner party or a large wedding, nothing is more annoying for a host or hostess than not to know how many people are attending. This can affect so many things: the size of venue, the number of tables, the catering, the wine and even the flowers, so good manners dictate a swift reply. Invitations should make clear whether you may bring a 'plus one' but, if not, never bring a friend, relation or partner unless you telephone your hosts to get the okay. I remember hosting a party where a man who should have known better turned up with a new girlfriend. I had seated him next to a single girl and, as room on the tables was very tight, it meant I had to rearrange several couples and my poor single guest ended up sitting next to a married man and another woman.

## BE CONFIDENT AT DINNER PARTIES

Dinner parties are a marvellous way of getting to know people, cementing business relationships and expanding your social circle. If you are a guest at a dinner party, your host will hope that you have something in common with the other guests, but you will need to develop the confidence to enjoy meeting new people and mixing with different groups.

The correct etiquette if you are a guest at a dinner party is as follows:

- When you are called to the table, don't linger to finish your drink or continue a fascinating conversation. Whoever has been preparing the food will not be amused to see it spoil or go cold. If nobody makes a move, stand up and head quietly for the door.
- Guests should wait to be seated by the host or hostess but, if told to sit anywhere, it is usual not to sit down next to your husband, wife or partner because the whole idea is to meet and talk to new people.

- Women sit first, but wait a moment in case grace is said, or any other ceremony observed.
- At a formal dinner, the hostess usually starts off by talking to the person on her left, so follow her lead.
- For a formal occasion the most important man sits on his hostess's right, and the next most important on her left. The most important woman sits on the host's right, and the next on his left.
- Subjects to avoid at parties are:
  - religion: this can be a private matter for many people
  - sex: this is better kept in the bedroom
  - money: to talk about how much money or how many possessions one has is considered crass in most western societies
  - illness and surgery: these are not topics most people want to hear about when they are eating.

It is now considered acceptable to start a conversation by complimenting your hosts upon their decor, food or wine, although it was not the thing to do until about the 1960s. It goes without saying that criticizing your hosts' decor, food or wine is an absolute 'no go', however garish, burnt or acid it might be.

## MIND YOUR TABLE MANNERS

Table etiquette is something that seems to worry many people. The object of eating is to enjoy the food. Eating should be effortless, elegant and discreet, allowing food to be eaten with the minimum of fuss so that conversation can flow. Good manners state that we don't put elbows on the table, we never speak with our mouths full, we don't wave cutlery in the air when speaking or between mouthfuls and we put cutlery on the plate in the 'crossed swords' position when we are not actually eating. When you have finished, put the cutlery tidily together placed at the '10.20' or '6.30' position.

If in doubt, use the cutlery from the outside in. A place setting for a typical five-course meal including soup, fish, main course, pudding and cheese would comprise the following on the right side of the place mat: a soup spoon, which is positioned on the outside, then – working inwards – the fish knife, the dinner knife, the pudding spoon and finally the cheese knife, which is next to the place mat. The bread knife (to be used for spreading butter on bread) can be placed on the side plate or on the outside of the soup spoon. On the left-hand side you will find the fish fork, large fork and finally the pudding fork, which is next to the place mat. There is a 'correct' way to hold cutlery when eating: the knife should be held in the right hand with index finger on the handle and the fork is held in the left hand with index finger on the handle above the tines.

The sweet course is called pudding, even if it is something as light as a soufflé. Dessert is the fruit that comes at the very end of a meal. Cheese is eaten before the pudding in some countries, so the table would be set accordingly and, in some hotels and houses, you may find the pudding spoon and fork above the place mat, but this is not strictly correct. Pudding is eaten with a spoon and fork or just a fork. Bread should be broken and a bite-size chunk then buttered if desired, and eaten.

## KNOW THE RULES ABOUT WINE AND GLASSWARE

When setting wine glasses, red wine is the largest, white wine glasses are slightly smaller and champagne is usually served in flutes. Always hold a wine glass by the stem, as holding the bowl of the glass will warm the liquid inside, changing the flavour. Water is served in a tumbler or a red wine glass. On the table, glasses should be placed on the right-hand side above the knives.

The glass you use first should be nearest to you, with the others slightly behind and the water glass somewhat to the left but easily accessible, in the hope that a glass of water is drunk with every glass of wine!

**Furthermore**

There are many excellent books on the subject of wine. When entertaining at home, go to a good wine merchant and tell them what you are planning to eat. The wine may cost a little more, but it will be well worth it. Again, give yourself time to try the wines; however well they are recommended, if you don't like them don't buy them. In a restaurant, if you are not sure what to order, ask the wine waiter what he or she would recommend to go with what people are eating.

1 2 3 4 5 6 7 8 9 10 11 12 13 14 15 16 17 18 19 20 21 22 23 24 25 26 27 28 29 30 31 32 33 34 35 36 37 38 39 40 41 42 43 44 45 46 47 48 49 50

### Putting it all together

Don't arrive earlier than the invitation says. The most important guests usually arrive last, so never turn up after the Queen! Rudely late is over 20 minutes, so a good rule of thumb is to arrive about ten minutes after the appointed time.

It should be down to your host to make introductions, but at a reasonable-sized gathering it may not be possible, at which point you need to take the initiative and introduce yourself. This is straightforward – simply state your name and, ideally, a snippet of information about yourself to encourage conversation. 'Hello, I'm Richard West and I've just moved into the area; do you live locally?' Or 'How do you do, I'm Joanna Green. Have you known our hosts (use their names here) long?'

It used to be the case that you would spend no longer than 15 minutes chatting to each guest. This is no longer true, but it is still not good manners to monopolize the prettiest or most amusing person in the room. And it is expected that you will move around the room, socializing with as many people as possible.

There is more information about how to join in and meet people at gatherings in Secret 27, 'Thrive in the corporate scene'.

# 27 Thrive in the corporate scene

“ *‘Outstanding leaders go out of their way to boost the self-esteem of their personnel. If people believe in themselves it’s amazing what they can accomplish.’* Sam Walton

“ *‘Business is not just doing deals; business is having great products, doing great engineering, and providing tremendous service to customers. Finally, business is a cobweb of human relationships.’* Ross Perot

“ *‘Get going. Move forward. Aim high. Plan a take-off. Don't just sit on the runway and hope someone will come along and push the airplane. It simply won’t happen. Change your attitude and gain some altitude. Believe me, you’ll love it up here.’* Donald Trump

“ *‘In the same way that I tend to make up my mind about people within 30 seconds of meeting them, I also make up my mind about whether a business proposal excites me within about 30 seconds of looking at it. I rely far more on gut instinct than researching huge amounts of statistics.’* Richard Branson

“ *‘Motivation is the art of getting people to do what you want them to do because they want to do it.’* Dwight D. Eisenhower

Confidence in the corporate arena is vital if you are going to thrive and prosper. The way you present yourself and deal with other people has been covered in previous secrets and it is one of your tools to become a confident communicator.



9 10 11 12 13 14 15 16 17 18 19 20 21 22 23 24 25 26 27 28 29 30 31 32 33 34 35 36 37 38 39 40 41 42 43 44 45 46 47 48 49 50

We all have weak points: for example, you might hate face-to-face confrontation, in which case write a letter or a memo, so that you can say what you mean without feeling you are going to lose control of the situation. Give yourself the time and space to think clearly and put your point across. If you find negotiating difficult, write down the outcome that you are looking for and stick to it. As we have seen in Secret 19, 'Use the power of a positive attitude', it is important to work on developing a positive mindset before you attempt an important negotiation. This will go a long way towards helping you project a confident manner.

Remember that both positivity and negativity are communicable and pass from person to person. If you can absorb the positive and disregard the negative, you will build your confidence. It is also important to build confidence in colleagues and staff. To give people a sense of their own worth enables them to develop their personality, achieve their true potential and work to their full capacity. Working as a team is also essential to the success of any organization and it is critical that everyone plays their part.

## MAKE A CONFIDENT FIRST IMPRESSION

To make a confident first impression, the most important factor is your visual appearance, so make sure that you are happy with your clothes and your grooming. These – and a smile – are the things others take in first.

The person to offer their hand first for a handshake is generally perceived to be the most assertive. The strength of contact can be an indicator of character. If no hand is offered in return, it may be because of religious barriers, a hygiene phobia or an attempt to snub you. If this happens to you, don't take it personally: put your hand down, smile and nod your head when you greet them and say your name. Keep your dignity and don't let it sap your self-assurance.

## MAKE EVERY DINNER A WINNER

A lot of money is wasted on corporate entertaining because not enough attention is paid to informing staff about the identity of key personnel. I remember talking to the CEO of a large insurance company in Kenya about an event he had been to, hosted by one of their biggest clients. He said he enjoyed the evening, met a few people and then went home. The next day he got a call asking why he hadn't attended the party. When he told them he had been there, they were devastated because the party had been thrown mainly for him and the chairman had wanted to say a personal thank you.

This sort of thing is surprisingly common so, if you want to be confident when running your office party, make sure everyone knows who the major players are, so they can be taken to the relevant table or introduced to the right people. Give everyone involved their names, a brief description of why they are there and somebody specific to look after them for the first half of the event.

If you are hosting a lunch or dinner, be aware that some people are not happy sitting with their back to an open door or space, so sit your client with their back to a wall, a divider or even some plants. A relaxing drink may be a good thing, but try to do the deal before any food is served. The blood supply concentrates in our stomachs when we have eaten in order to digest the food, so the brain tends to be ignored, which is not good when decisions have to be made! There's a school of thought that says a round table is less confrontational than a square one; if your table is square and you are worried about it, don't sit opposite your client, but to one side.

## MAKE SURE YOUR IRON FIST IS IN A VELVET GLOVE

There's a big difference between confidence and arrogance. Over-confidence or superiority is often displayed by the way someone sits. This could be with hands clasped behind the head; or leaning back in the chair with legs outstretched and ankles crossed. A prospective employer or future client adopting this position could well be playing for effect to see how you react to such rudeness. An arrogant person doesn't make a good manager. If you tell, rather than ask people to do something and control your staff with a heavy hand, life will not be easy for anyone. The iron fist in the velvet glove is a better approach. It is important not to be a pushover, but politeness and good manners are highly significant in people management.

Examples of an arrogant approach might be:

- 'Get this into the post by five o'clock.'
- 'The reason we are going to proceed this way is because it is the best way.'
- 'There is a departmental meeting this afternoon – make sure you're there!'

An alternative approach might be:

- 'Please make sure this gets into the post by five o'clock.'
- 'I can see you have a very good point, but the reason we are going to proceed this way is because it is the best strategy for the whole department.'
- 'There is a meeting at two o'clock. It is important, so I look forward to seeing you all there.'

Those examples may seem painfully obvious, but can you honestly say you have never spoken aggressively under duress? It is important to realize the effect that this sort of approach might have on employees or colleagues.

## Putting it all together

Recognize the value of a positive first impression and make sure you are happy with how you look and the impact you are going to create. This takes prior planning, so be prepared! Diplomacy and good manners are not a sign of weakness and will always win the day, so 'ask' rather than 'tell' when requesting someone to do something. Compliment others whenever possible, on appearance as well as results. Motivate by encouraging new ideas.

Criticize constructively, pointing out where things have gone wrong and give guidance on how to improve them. It is important to do it in private if feasible, to avoid any embarrassment. Praise as much as possible; don't think people 'know what you mean' because they don't unless you tell them. You will lack confidence at times but, if you make the most of your good points and forgive yourself the weak ones, you can do a great deal to boost your morale and build self-assurance.

Whatever you are going to do, whether it is organizing an office party, making a speech or negotiating a deal, take time to prepare. Give yourself as much time as possible to find out about the personnel, the background, the venue and the situation. Make sure nobody has too much to drink when entertaining and try to 'do the deal before the meal'!

1 2 3 4 5 6 7 8 9 10 11 12 13 14 15 16 17 18 19 20 21 22 23 24 25 26

28 29 30 31 32 33 34 35 36 37 38 39 40 41 42 43 44 45 46 47 48 49 50

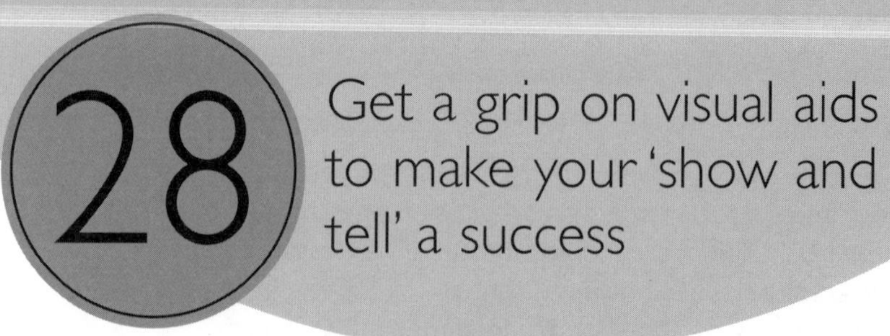

# 28 Get a grip on visual aids to make your 'show and tell' a success

*'The most truthful part of a newspaper is the advertisements.'*
Thomas Jefferson

*'Doing business without advertising is like winking at a girl in the dark. You know what you are doing but nobody else does.'*
Stuart Henderson Britt, Marketing Management and Administrative Action

*'I don't know the rules of grammar. If you're trying to persuade people to do something, or buy something, it seems to me you should use their language.'* David Ogilvy

*'Tell me and I'll forget; show me and I may remember; involve me and I'll understand.'* Chinese proverb

*'My Life is My Message.'* Mahatma Gandhi

When you are giving a speech, you are advertising yourself, a product or a service. As with an advertising campaign, there are all sorts of tools you can use to make your speech as targeted and stimulating as possible. Along with PowerPoint, video and a variety of visual aids, other vital elements of making your performance a success are lecterns, autocue, screens and microphones. Assessing the height and depth of a stage should also be part of the preparation before you make your speech.

Remember that the visuals are there only to support what you say – you are the presenter and you are giving the speech. A PowerPoint presentation is not the speech itself. The audience will be paying more attention to what you *say* than to the visual aids, which should be there merely to give the audience an idea of the structure, with a few key words on each slide rather than long sentences.

Using a microphone can be problematic if you haven't rehearsed beforehand. How close should you hold it? Is it omnidirectional? Should you have a radio mic? It all depends on how you make your presentation. If you like to walk as you talk, you will need a radio mic so that you have freedom of movement. If, on the other hand, you like the comfort of a lectern that you can hold on to and from which you can access your notes, then you need a fixed microphone. There is no one size fits all.

**Furthermore**

The right music can create a wonderful atmosphere and if you aren't a natural comedian, a few humorous slides can add a real lift to a presentation. Look at TV commercials for ideas. Cartoons can also really help push your message home, but it is you who is the expert and whom your audience has come to hear, so make sure you are the star of the show!

## USE VISUAL AIDS IN YOUR PRESENTATION

If you are using PowerPoint or other visual aids, it is imperative to test the equipment as soon as you get to the venue. If it is your gear and you have tried it out the night before, try it again, as delicate equipment is notorious for developing faults at the last minute. If your presentation is on a memory stick or your phone, then try out the laptop and projector in the hall or room where you are presenting. Is the projector easy to focus? Is your presentation properly lined up? Nothing makes a professional presentation look amateur like a false start or images that are fuzzy or out of focus. Even if you take your own equipment, it is not a bad idea to have everything backed up on a memory stick, just in case of disasters!

When deciding how to style your PowerPoint slides, be aware that a white background with dark font is the easiest for your audience to read. If you use a dark background for some slides, you obviously need to use a light font for the text. Bullet points should be three lines or four at the most; too much text is distracting for the audience. They should keep listening to you rather than get lost trying to make sense of too much information on the slide. All visuals are there to help rather than *compete* with the presenter.

The number of slides you use depends on the complexity of the speech, as does the number of images. You may need graphs to support what you are saying, and these should be dynamic but simple.

Remember that many people in your audience may not give you their full attention unless your presentation is lively and varied. (They may be tired, sneakily checking their emails or even asleep!) Videos can enhance the presentation as well as giving you a breather, but they must be well produced with excellent sound quality as well as not being too long.

## USE TRICKS OF THE TRADE TO GET YOUR MESSAGE ACROSS

You are selling something to your audience when you make a presentation or a speech, and confident speakers use all the tricks of the trade to get their message across. To get ideas, look at adverts in the paper to help give you headlines. Analyse commercials on TV and the radio to see how powerfully they can transmit a message in 15 or 30 seconds.

Before any presentation, you must leave yourself enough time to assess the facilities. It is no good finding that the sound system is faulty just as you are about to start your speech. This will sap your confidence, so you need to know how close to hold the mic, whether you can turn your head from side to side and still be heard and when it is going to 'pop'. ('Popping' is when you are too close and everyone can hear a pop on every consonant.)

Every room has a different ambience and every microphone is different, so don't think that just because you have used the same equipment before it will be the same in a different venue. Take time over the sound check. If the sound isn't right, the audience will not enjoy it. You need to make sure your message is audible whatever the size of the audience, and that means no crackling, no echo and no distorted sound.

## TAKE TO THE STAGE

Stages come in all shapes and sizes. As with everything else, if you can try out your stage beforehand, it is time well spent. If there are spotlights, you need to know where to stand so that they are shining on you. If you are in shadow or they are casting an unflattering light, it can be distracting for the audience. This is especially true if you like to walk around as you speak. It is also as well to know that the sound is the same on all parts of the stage. If there is a large screen as a backdrop to the stage, you need to be aware of the projector in order to avoid walking through the beam. If you are using a laser pointer, check its batteries and its trajectory beforehand.

Have your notes typed clearly and in a large enough font to allow you to read them easily, and mark the script to remind you when visuals come up. Practise with the remote control if you are changing your own slides – it gives a bad impression if you are talking about slide four and we are still seeing slide two. It can also knock you off your stride, so make sure you know that everything works if you want to feel really confident. If someone else is changing the slides for you, work out beforehand what signal you will give them. A nod of the head is less annoying for your audience than constantly saying 'Next slide please!'

If you are using a speech prompter, you have to use a lectern, since that is where the glass will be placed. The monitor is placed under the lectern and it sends a mirror image to a clear piece of glass on the top. To the audience, it looks as though the speaker has memorized their speech, but in fact he or she is reading it. However, to make reading an autocue look natural you need to rehearse, especially if you have two screens, so that you can look from one side of the audience to the other without losing your place. You also have to have a consistent reading speed for the operator, as it can be a nightmare for them if you constantly speed up then slow down. The faster you read, the faster they will scroll the text, so don't let your presentation become like an express train out of control!

It may sound obvious, but make sure that you can get on and off the stage easily. Some stages don't have proper steps, which can present a real hazard for people in high heels and a tight skirt. If you feel the steps are not adequate and you can't find a box or something to make them higher, ensure that someone will be available to give you a hand off the stage.

### Putting it all together

Once again, preparation is all. This is especially true if you are using any mechanical equipment, so make sure you test it beforehand. Talk to the autocue or speech prompter operator to discuss the content, and try to keep your speed fairly even. Make sure your notes are legible and don't have too many confusing alterations. Use a visual element when you want to make a particular point – pictures talk to people. For inspiration, study adverts in the papers, on radio and on TV to help you make your message sharp and focused. If you are going to use music or video clips, make sure they are royalty free, otherwise you could be landed with a hefty bill from the Performing Rights Society or film or TV watchdogs.

Visual aids are there to help the audience understand the message; they shouldn't be used simply as a prompt for the speaker. Having said that, speakers (and their audiences) find that slides enliven a presentation. Graphs, charts and diagrams can be used to explain complex ideas, using PowerPoint or similar software. Size of text on your slides can vary, but make sure it is compatible with the size of the screen and the size of the room. At the end of the presentation, distribute handouts that are a combination of your PowerPoint slides and your notes.

# 29 Speak off the cuff with ease and enthusiasm

> *'In order to succeed, your desire for success should be greater than your fear of failure.'* Bill Cosby

> *'Success is not final, failure is not fatal; it is the courage to continue that counts.'* Winston Churchill

> *'Always be yourself, express yourself, have faith in yourself, do not go out and look for a successful personality and duplicate it.'* Bruce Lee

> *'Fear of danger is ten thousand times more terrifying than danger itself.'* Daniel Defoe

> *'It is just when ideas are lacking that a phrase is most welcome.'* Goethe

Most people find it difficult to make an impromptu speech. The idea of someone suddenly asking you to 'say a few words' at a birthday party or an office leaving do, for instance, can be a daunting prospect, to say the least. Until I used the tips I am going to give you, I know my mind would go horribly blank. However, there is a failsafe way to make this task a success: past, present and future are the three magic words. Using this format, I can speak for at least ten minutes on any topic you care to name. All you have to do is take a subject, look at its past, discuss where it is now and what is likely to happen with it in the future.

You can use this technique to wax lyrical on an inanimate object, a project, an organization, a relative, a friend, a colleague or even a favourite pet. The good thing about being asked to give an impromptu talk is that they don't have to last long and people's expectations are not high. They are just grateful that you will do it and they marvel at your confidence and seemingly effortless expertise.

**Past, present and future are the three magic words in speechmaking.**

## TAKE YOUR AUDIENCE INTO THE PAST

When someone challenges me to show them how to make this format work, I use whatever object is nearest to hand to demonstrate. Let's take a drinking glass, for example. In the past, what type of vessel did we drink from? I could go as far back as I like into the past.

It might be a vessel carefully carved from the antler of a deer that was killed to feed the family in Europe or North America. How long did to take to carve it and what would the water, mead or wine taste like? I don't know the answer, but I can let my imagination run and inspire my audience enough to imagine drinking out of that vessel with me. Would it have a whiff of deer, tainting the flavour of the drink until it had been used and washed for some months or years? Would it crack if I poured boiling water into it or if it got caught by the frost on a very cold night?

I could perhaps talk about a ceramic cup from Roman times and go into detail about the life that cup might have had in a Roman garrison in cold, damp Chester near where I live, and the battles it might have seen. I might talk about a coconut shell used to collect water in an oasis in the desert, surrounded by camels and perhaps beautiful Arabian steeds. I can talk about the wonders of Venetian glass and the glass blowers of the fifteenth century. I could weave a tale about a gold goblet used by a king.

That one little word 'past' has led me into the land of my imagination and storytelling, and that is what a good, inspiring speech is all about. If, however, we are talking about a real person – somebody who is in the room – one has to be a little more circumspect, especially if the past is something they would rather forget. You can still mention it, of course, but go back to safe ground. Talk about school days, shared hobbies, holidays or projects you have done together, rather than the salacious details of past liaisons or corporate disasters!

## BRING THE AUDIENCE INTO THE PRESENT

Sticking with my glass, my job now becomes much easier. I can talk about all the different glasses we use today and when we use them: wine glasses, whisky tumblers, cocktail glasses, beer tankards, champagne flutes, brandy balloons, to mention a few. You can tell your own stories about summer nights sipping champagne overlooking the Aegean Sea or drinking Guinness in December after winning a rugby match.

By the time you have described all the occasions when you have used glasses and the passion you are now feeling about them and the wonderful beverages that filled them, you should be able to talk until midnight! All you need to do is think outside the box and let your passion flow.

When talking about a colleague, you can say what they are doing now and bring in any interesting (but not embarrassing) snippet of information that the audience may be unaware of.

## TALK TO YOUR AUDIENCE ABOUT THE FUTURE

Now we come into the realm of storytelling, as who knows what will happen in the future? Today we are drinking out of vessels made of glass, plastic, ceramic, steel, pewter, silver, gold, porcelain, cardboard (who would have thought it 50 years ago), leather and so on, but what of the future? Will we invent cups made of new substances that will heat or cool liquid simply by pressing a button on their side? Will everything be biodegradable to eliminate waste or will we hark back to the more traditional materials that have served us well for years? No one knows, but we can have fun guessing.

Whoever you are speaking about, whether it is someone young such as a niece or nephew or a contemporary such as a business associate, you can mention what *they* will be doing in the future. Your niece or nephew may be going travelling or to university, or have landed a first job. Your associate may have gained promotion, be moving on or retiring, so you can wish them the best of luck and propose a toast.

**Putting it all together**

A failsafe way to bring information from your own experience and speak for at least ten minutes 'off the cuff' is to use this format: past, present and future. Give yourself at least six or seven minutes to prepare and write down relevant points. This is obviously easier if you have gone to the trouble of acquiring a wealth of up-to-date knowledge, have read widely and developed a good vocabulary and a vivid imagination, as discussed in previous secrets in this book.

Some people find impromptu speeches easier to give than others, but we can all do it, even those of us who feel initially nervous about it. We just need confidence and a few minutes to gather our thoughts. However, never offer to speak, even if your arm is severely twisted, if you have had too much to drink because that road can lead to disaster!

# 30 Keep your confidence levels up when age catches up with you

> *'Anyone who stops learning is old, whether at twenty or eighty. Anyone who keeps learning stays young. The greatest thing in life is to keep your mind young.'* Henry Ford

> *'An archaeologist is the best husband a woman can have. The older she gets the more interested he is in her.'* Agatha Christie

> *'There is a fountain of youth: it is your mind, your talents, the creativity you bring to your life and the lives of people you love. When you learn to tap this source, you will truly have defeated age.'* Sophia Loren

> *'Do not regret growing older. It is a privilege denied to many.'* Anon.

> *'A woman cannot choose her features at twenty; but it is her own fault if she is not beautiful at sixty.'* Anon.

When we are young we never really think about growing old. Some young people have a tendency to dismiss the elderly as another species, but the truth is that – if we are lucky – we will all live to grow old. I never know the age of my readers, but I try to cater for everybody. The secrets in this book show you how to be a confident communicator when talking to people in any age group, in many different situations. Most of us can look forward to living more than the traditional 'three score years and ten' nowadays, and we will remain healthier and more active than our grandparents did.

9 10 11 12 13 14 15 16 17 18 19 20 21 22 23 24 25 26 27 28 29 30 31 32 33 34 35 36 37 38 39 40 41 42 43 44 45 46 47 48 49 50

It is how we cope with the advancing years that is important. The number of people living to be 100 is increasing every year. My uncle John is now 101 and still lives on his own. We as a family are very close and I try to see him at least once a week when I am in the country, but he also has wonderful neighbours who look out for him and invite him round to watch football and snooker on TV, so that he can have a shared experience. This is vital in keeping him mentally agile so that he doesn't shrink into a world of his own and fall prey to loneliness and isolation. Loneliness is a killer because people literally give up the will to live if they don't talk to another human being from one week to the next. It is almost impossible to believe that this can happen in 'civilized' countries like the UK and USA. Ironically, it would not happen in most countries in Africa or many parts of Asia, where the elderly are venerated for their wisdom and insight and the older generation lives with the family as they become infirm or lonely and often help look after the grandchildren.

## USE IT OR LOSE IT: KEEP YOUR BODY AND MIND ACTIVE

As we get older, we can lose our confidence. After retirement from a long career, people can easily feel lost and left out, and think that they have little or nothing to offer the world. Many parents can feel the same sense of loss of purpose when their children leave home, if bringing up children has been their main focus. While family life is of paramount importance, it is essential not to live our lives through our children or, indeed, to find our identity solely through our job. Even if you are lucky enough to enjoy work that you can do indefinitely without having to retire, that doesn't mean you shouldn't make time for family, friends and hobbies.

This is the secret of confident communication as you get older: you need to keep your body active and your mind alert. Remaining in good health is vitally important. If you start to lose your hearing, or your eyesight is not as good as it was, this will affect your ability to communicate and you will feel more isolated, so it is vital to do something about it. Many men and women put off getting a hearing aid, probably from reasons of vanity, but nothing is more isolating than not being able to hear. You cannot join in conversations properly and people (especially family!) start getting tetchy if they have to keep answering the same questions and repeating themselves because you haven't heard what they said.

**Furthermore**

Do yourself and your friends a favour and investigate your hearing if you are finding that you have to ask people to repeat themselves and that you are turning up the volume of the TV more than before. The quality of hearing aids has greatly improved and you can hardly even see them. It is the same with eyesight: get it checked regularly so that you can keep driving and keep your independence.

## TRY SOMETHING NEW

If you have lost confidence with the passing years, it is not always easy to regain it. Keep your brain nimble by reading as much as you can and learning new hobbies if possible. Here are some ideas for activities to try.

**Bridge** This is a great game for people of all ages, because it makes you think clearly and deliberately and it is also very sociable. Some players take it extremely seriously while others just want a good game and time to chat and make friends. You need four people to play, and you can learn at a bridge club, which might be at someone's home or in a village hall. These clubs take place during the daytime and in the evenings, so you can choose the time of day that suits you as well as the level of skill of people you want to play with.

**Computers and the Internet** Learning how to use the Internet is essential if you want to keep in touch with the younger generation, shop online, talk to people over Skype and keep up with what is going on. Libraries and colleges run courses and you can pick up second-hand computers for practically nothing.

Another way of keeping the mind active and meeting like-minded people is to join a book club or learn to paint.

If you own a dog, you will know that walking is one of the best ways to keep fit. Alternatively, join a walking group or do a charity walk. Golf can also be a boost to both health and confidence – it needs skill to play well. These days you don't even have to be a member of a particular club; you can just pay green fees and play to the level that suits you.

Another way to gain confidence is to update your wardrobe, your hairstyle and, for women, your make-up. If you dress the same way you have dressed for the last 20 years, people will perceive you as someone who is not 'up with the times' and therefore with not much to offer intellectually.

## GET OUT INTO THE WORLD AND GIVE SOMETHING BACK

Don't wait for people to come to you – go out and meet the world! Show interest in others and ask them questions, especially the younger generation and any grandchildren. Find out what they like in their world and do your homework. If you have never seen *Star Wars* or *Spiderman*, get a DVD and watch at least some of it so that you can have a good conversation.

As people get older, they sometimes lose interest in what others are doing and want to talk about themselves and the old days. While this is very interesting to a degree, we must all take an interest in the present and look forward. There is no point in living if we are not interested in the future, even if it might not affect us directly.

Give something back by starting a group or helping out in an existing one. Keep in touch with as many people as you can and offer yourself as a volunteer. This is a marvellous way of giving back to society, and it gives you the opportunity to meet others and give their lives a sense of purpose. For example, groups exist to help the housebound get out and about, and take them shopping or to other activities.

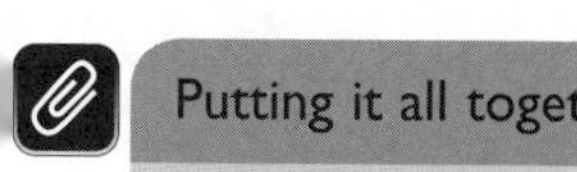

## Putting it all together

Keeping as fit and as supple as possible will help you to carry on doing the things you always used to do, which will give you confidence. Eating well is also a must if you are to remain hale and hearty. Walk as much as you can and use the stairs whenever possible. Limit the amount of time you spend sitting, because the more you sit the more weight you will carry and the less energy you will have.

It is also important to keep up with world affairs so that you have an up-to-date opinion and can contribute to political discussion and debates. Learn new skills and take up new hobbies. Again, it is a great way to meet new people. Pets are another way of reducing loneliness. Cats make good pets because they are very self-sufficient – you can put in a cat-flap or litter tray and leave them food and water for a day. Unlike cats, dogs need regular exercise and training, and dog-training classes are another way of making new friends.

Keeping your clothing, hair and general appearance up to date will give you confidence and help you communicate more easily. Try to think of others and look outwards into the world.

# 31 Offer telling tributes in your important speeches

> *'Be sincere; be brief; be seated.'* Franklin D. Roosevelt

> *'A speech is like a woman's skirt: it needs to be long enough to cover the subject matter but short enough to hold the audience's attention.'* Anon.

> *'The life of the dead is placed in the memory of the living. So, speak good words, and let the dead rest in peace.'* Cicero

> *'A toast before we go into battle. True love. In whatever shape or form it may come. May we all in our dotage be proud to say, "I was adored once, too."'*
> Gareth, in the film *Four Weddings and a Funeral*

> *'The fame of heroes owes little to the extent of their conquests and all to the success of the tributes paid to them.'*
> Jean Genet

It is likely that many of us will be asked at least once in our lives to speak at a birthday party, a wedding or a leaving or retirement party, or to give a eulogy at a funeral service. To make these important speeches a success, time has to be spent on research. Although a good starting point is to use the structure of past, present and future, as discussed for impromptu speeches in Secret 29, when you have more time to prepare you need to talk to the people who have stories to tell and relevant information about the subject.

The structure of these speeches is vital and here, above all, you need to bear in mind what your audience would like to know and is of interest to them, rather than what you want to tell them. Never keep your speech a secret from everyone: read it beforehand to someone you trust, who will tell you if it is a little too long or over the top. Ten to fifteen minutes is long enough for any speech at these occasions.

**Furthermore**

In a large space, having a good PA system is a must, as if guests can't hear they will switch off and your carefully rehearsed speech will lose its impact.

## MAKE A PERFECT WEDDING SPEECH

Weddings are wonderful but they can be spoilt by boring, lengthy or drunken speeches. In the past, a relative or an old family friend would have given the toast to the bride, but now it is usually the father, or sometimes the mother, who talks about their beautiful daughter, and then there are the groom's and the best man's speeches as well. It is important that all these speeches be objective, kind and fairly succinct.

**The father of the bride's speech** (or whoever proposes the health of the bride) should include some stories about her childhood and her achievements but they shouldn't be boastful. As a parent, you may think she is the best woman ever to have been born, but not everyone might agree if they have daughters of their own! Pick out things that show a different side to her personality or things that aren't generally known. Far too many wedding speeches describe the bride's life in endless detail from the day she was born – when she first crawled and got her first teeth, her first day at school, her numerous sporting triumphs as well as all her academic achievements – until the guests are dying of boredom and the bride is dying of embarrassment.

**Furthermore**

Since wedding guests' attention spans tend to be short, especially when drink has been taken, don't have too many speeches and don't let them go on too long or you will have the embarrassing problem of people talking rather than listening or drinking too much so they start heckling.

**The best man's speech** should not be an opportunity to tell the world embarrassing stories and 'in jokes' that most of the guests aren't able to follow. This is bad manners and leads to instant boredom for most of the audience. Remember that the groom's parents, siblings and the bride herself may not be pleased to hear about embarrassing drunken escapades. Keep these for the stag night. If you are using video clips, by all means include funny clips and stories but, again, tell us or show us something of interest to everyone that won't embarrass him or us too much. Keep it short!

Speeches are given before the meal at a number of weddings now so that the wedding party can relax and enjoy the occasion. It also means there is more of a chance that the best man will be in a fit state to be able to read his notes and not indulge himself ad-libbing!

**The bridegroom's speech** includes a toast to the bridesmaids, to thank them for looking after his beautiful bride and to say how lovely they look. He can also talk about his new wife and their future together, but not go on and on because 'she is worth it'. Although it is the bride and groom's special day, it should also be special for the guests and, if speeches overrun, it can affect timings for the caterers, the band, the DJ and also for guests who are asked only for the latter part of the evening.

## GIVE A GREAT BIRTHDAY SPEECH

It is usually at a 'significant' birthday that speeches are given – an 18th or a 21st birthday party. If you are writing the speech, make it a tribute to the birthday boy or girl and not an ego trip for you. That may sound harsh, but it is surprising how many people get carried away with their own wit and ingenuity and completely lose sight of what the tribute is in aid of. As with wedding speeches, be aware of older family members who may be present. Edit the jokes in your head when you are writing the speech and, if Granny wouldn't like it, don't use it!

The type of event – which might be a dinner, a night at a club or a dance in a marquee or large house – will dictate the length of the speech. Keep it very short in a club where the noise level is likely to be high: just a few compliments to the birthday boy or girl are enough before the toast. This is usually just a cue for the cake to be brought in and leading everyone in a rousing chorus of 'Happy birthday'.

At big private parties, video is now a regular part of the tribute. Once more, if you know the older generation are a bit stuffy, your birthday girl might not enjoy seeing too much of her flesh on display or a picture of her in a less than flattering pose. Boys can also feel sick with embarrassment if they are caught on camera in one of their more foolish moments. Ten to fifteen minutes is long enough for any birthday speech, video or slide show – remember, the object of the event is for people to enjoy the refreshments, mix and dance if there is music.

## GIVE A HEARTFELT EULOGY

If you are a good speaker, you may be asked to give a eulogy at a funeral or memorial service, even if you did not know the deceased particularly well. It is a great honour to be asked to give a tribute and the speech requires careful preparation. The family wants someone to give the correct amount of gravitas and sensitivity; they also want the tribute to be delivered with clarity and confidence. This can be difficult, especially if the person was a relation or great friend and you are feeling sad yourself. You have to try to focus on that person and how they would want to be remembered.

Start by talking to the family and close friends and asking questions. These cannot be too intimate but should encourage the surviving family to think back and remember the things about the person that made them smile. This is a time when all the things you didn't know about that person can come out and their achievements can be lauded.

The speech is unlike a tribute to the living because the family is primarily grieving rather than celebrating and the person has no right of reply, so it must be accurate and tasteful, with no nasty surprises. However, more people these days see a funeral or memorial service as a thanksgiving for the life that has ended and some families want a more celebratory approach, with the mourners wearing colourful clothes rather than the traditional black. This means that the tone of the tribute can be more light-hearted, but it is important to discuss this thoroughly first and offer to show the nearest and dearest the speech beforehand.

### Putting it all together

As with any speech, tributes need thorough preparation. Start preparing early, not on the day, as I have seen more than one best man try unsuccessfully to do. An ill-prepared speech will be rambling, repetitive and boring, so use all the techniques we have discussed in Secrets 21 to 24. If you are showing pictures or video, make sure the equipment is working properly and the sound is of high quality. Vet your jokes so that they are appropriate and funny to everyone, not just a chosen few. Above all, stay sober until after the speech! You make think a bit of alcohol will sooth your nerves, but usually it serves to deaden the memory and loosen the tongue, to the embarrassment of all concerned.

Just as you do when you are when making a formal presentation, you need to be able to read and assess your audience. You are not the important one, your audience is. Your tribute is a vital part of the wedding, birthday or memorial service and if you mess up, you mess up for everyone.

# 32 Sharpen your ability to look, listen and learn

*'Joy in looking and comprehending is nature's most beautiful gift.'* Albert Einstein

*'One of the most sincere forms of respect is actually listening to what others have to say.'* Bryant H. McGill

*'It's pretty simple, pretty obvious: that people's first impressions of people are really a big mistake.'* Vincent D'Onofrio

*'We don't know where our first impressions come from or precisely what they mean, so we don't always appreciate their fragility.'* Malcolm Gladwell

*'If your actions inspire others to dream more, learn more, do more and become more, you are a leader.'* John Quincy Adams

How often do you notice your environment when you walk into your workplace? They say that we should see ourselves as others see us, but do you ever see your environment through the eyes of your clients and customers? Do you wonder what your reception says about you? Does it match your mission statement?

First impressions are vital; just as we do with people, we make up our minds about things within 20 seconds of first seeing them. If your company motto is 'Quality is at the heart of everything we do' but your reception has a surly woman on the desk and there are dirty smudges on the skirting boards

9 10 11 12 13 14 15 16 17 18 19 20 21 22 23 24 25 26 27 28 39 30 31 32 33 34 35 36 37 38 39 40 41 42 43 44 45 46 47 48 49 50

and grubby marks round the door handles or light switches, it belies your mission statement. If you don't pay attention to the small details, it implies that you might not pay attention to the bigger ones.

In these highly competitive times, a candid and thorough audit of people and places will help identify areas of concern that might just be putting you one step *behind* the competition. It has been scientifically proven that colour, light, decor and use of space can strongly affect the productivity of employees. If a particular department frequently has people going off sick, it is as well to check the environment. What is the lighting like? Is there adequate ventilation? Is it a nice place to be? Ensuring that people are able to work comfortably and in pleasant surroundings, with equipment that works properly, shows respect and consideration; unkempt or dirty surroundings and machinery that breaks down show the reverse.

**Furthermore**

The work environment, as much as your products, shows whether a company really pays attention to detail in all areas of its operations, and it has a direct effect on the productivity of the workforce, leading to either beneficial or detrimental effects on the 'bottom line'. The secret is in maximizing the business environment.

When planning a workspace, we often overlook the effect on people of our surroundings; too much emphasis is put on the 'look' rather than the practicalities and conditions. In this secret we will cover what you need to look for when setting up your workspace in order to ensure maximum productivity for you and your staff. To be a confident communicator, it is essential that you know that everyone you work with feels comfortable in their work setting. This not only reflects your values but also enables everyone to be happy in their workplace so that you can all be proud of your business environment. People are the organization and as a consequence will reflect company values.

## LOOK AT YOUR WORK ENVIRONMENT THROUGH OTHERS' EYES

Look at your environment carefully and try to see it from an outsider's viewpoint, as if you have never entered the building before. What would your first impression be? Make a list of the things that might need changing and what you could do to make it better. Is there enough light? If there is not much natural light, it is possible to have daylight lighting, which is known to give people more energy and help combat 'sad syndrome' in the winter.

The space between desks in an open-plan office can make a big difference to workers' comfort. If you sit behind a desk for hours at a time, your workstation needs to be properly designed. Proper office ergonomics, including correct chair height, sufficient equipment spacing and good desk posture can help you and your workforce stay healthy at work, preventing neck and back pain or sore wrists and fingers.

Green plants give any workplace a lift and they can also combat the negative ions given off by computers. If you want more colour, which always brightens the office as well as lifting the soul, gerbera daisies are the thing, or think about giving an air-cleansing spider plant or peace lily a home on your workstation.

Look at your colleagues and employees. Read their body talk and the expressions on their faces. Do they look happy? Are their shoulders hunched and do they look bored or disinterested? If so, you need to do something about it. Unless you really *look* at your environment and the people in it, you might not notice any of these things.

## LISTEN TO OTHERS TO UNDERSTAND THEIR WORLD

It is vital to enter into someone else's 'biosphere' if you are to listen properly; showing someone that you are keen to understand their world helps that person feel empathy. If you are a manager, listening is a vital part of your job if you are to get the best out of your workforce. It's hard to find silence in today's world to listen to anyone, but listening to another person requires more than just your ears. You not only have to listen, you have to be *seen* to be listening; otherwise the other person will not feel they are making contact with you. Obviously, we all use our ears to listen, but you need to listen so intently and patiently that the other person can '*hear* themselves think'.

To be an effective listener. you need to:

- sit up straight, block out internal distractions and ignore external distractions like phone calls
- maintain 'comfortable' eye contact
- use friendly, encouraging, open, non-verbal gestures
- give verbal encouragement
- take short notes if appropriate to make sure you remember everything.

This method of effective listening helps you to understand what motivates your employee or colleague and encourages them to become more forthcoming. It builds trust. Within a nurturing environment, employees will gain confidence faster and learn to perform better within a group. For successful, confident communication, it is essential to talk less and listen more.

## LEARN FROM WHAT YOU HAVE SEEN AND HEARD

Learn what you have seen and heard and then analyse those learning points. Look at your products or services from your customers' and competitors' points of view; what can this teach you? Think back and learn from things your clients or customers have said; make a list of things that need addressing and take action.

Learn to value your staff, customers and clients and always keep your promises – if you say you are going to do something, do it and let people know when you have done it. Learn to build rapport and find genuine common ground as well as opportunities for co-operation with both employees and customers. Learn from employee requirements and empower your workforce by supporting and nurturing them with appropriate training. Start ideas forums so that everyone can have their say and new ideas, possible changes in working practices and 'out of the box' suggestions can be aired.

## Putting it all together

Looking analytically at your staff, your work environment and your products and services will help you keep one step ahead of the competition. We know that colour, light, decor and use of space can have beneficial or detrimental effects on the 'bottom line' because they affect the productivity of employees. If a particular department frequently has people going off sick, it is as well to check the environment. Look also at your competitors' products and premises, to see what you can learn from them. Having an open-door policy to allow colleagues and employees to talk, and then listening intently to what they say and taking action where appropriate, will improve productivity.

Building rapport with staff will create trust and confidence that you are reliable and will respect confidences, especially when you are listening to complaints and grievances. Concentrate on the individual when listening, without evaluating until you have had time to carefully think things through. Enhance rapport through the subtle matching of body language when trying to understand another person's feelings, viewpoints and drives. Showing that you are genuinely interested in your employees and their world will also help you determine how to move your organization forward. Ask powerful and probing questions. Ascertain the state of mind of your workforce and clients; this can help stop problems before they start. Encourage ideas and innovation and listen so intently that the other person can 'hear themselves think'.

1 2 3 4 5 6 7 8 9 10 11 12 13 14 15 16 17 18 19 20 21 22 23 24 25 26 27 28 29 30 31 32 33 34 35 36 37 38 39 40 41 42 43 44 45 46 47 48 49 50

# 33 Hone your workplace communication

> *'Much unhappiness has come into the world because of bewilderment and things left unsaid.'* Fyodor Dostoyevsky

> *'Constantly talking isn't necessarily communicating.'* Charlie Kaufman

> *'Electric communication will never be a substitute for the face of someone who with their soul encourages another person to be brave and true.'* Charles Dickens

> *'The greatest problem in communication is the illusion that it has been accomplished.'* George Bernard Shaw

> *'Courage is what it takes to stand up and speak. Courage is also what it takes to sit down and listen.'* Winston Churchill

You want something done – and you want it done now – so surely the best way to achieve your aim is to instruct your staff to do it? Not necessarily: this method takes the thoughts of only one individual, but the work of others who don't necessarily share that vision, to reach an objective.

**Furthermore**

As we have seen, the way to effective communication is by talking *and* listening. The more time you spend listening, the more you build a strong and valuable relationship with your staff. The more you listen, the more you will find out how your employees and colleagues think and operate and what they are capable of. This will enable you to release talent and potential and boost productivity. You will be able to delegate more and supervise less.

When you employ someone, it is essential to define the job, the responsibilities and the degree of discipline expected right at the start, then everybody knows where they are. But if you are an employee, how do you communicate with your bosses as well as your colleagues? How do you put new ideas forward or make sure you are heard if you have a complaint? Building rapport with those you work with is vital if you are going to succeed as a team, so when people feel valued as well as wholly involved with their work, there'll be higher productivity and profitability and lower levels of staff turnover.

We need to use empathy in our interactions with others to accomplish successful communication. 'This is how I see the situation…' 'This is what I believe and why…' 'This is what I want and why…' You need to be sure in your convictions. If you sound unsure, nobody will believe you and you will lose credibility. It is essential that you have a firm, but informed, opinion. 'In my opinion we should do x, y and z, and if we do, the outcome will be…'

The choice of 'I' or 'we' can have a significant effect on how confident and competent we sound. Women tend to use 'we' and apologize more, even though when they say 'I'm sorry' it is often meant as an expression of concern rather than a statement of apology.

## SHARE THOUGHTS AND IDEAS TO IMPROVE COMMUNICATION

Whether you are a manager or an employee, effective communication means sharing thoughts and ideas and then acting on them collectively. This 'mentoring' form of management is often far more successful than the traditional command, control and coercion management style. It has advantages for both management and employees and should lead to accelerated learning and development, increased self-awareness and self-discipline because employees are encouraged to think for themselves and air thoughts and ideas. The provision of a sounding board and constructive feedback brings increased self-confidence and self-esteem as well as greater creativity and enhanced problem solving.

As a manager, ask yourself whether your employees work *for* you or *with* you. Picture a swing door separating you, the manager, from your staff. You can 'push' the door, effectively pushing your ideas and thoughts on to your workforce, or you can 'pull' the door, inviting their thoughts and ideas. You are still the one with the goals, the strategies and the vision, but surely it would be good to know what your staff think? If they are not aware of the company's goals, how can they help achieve them? There's also a fair chance that they might have contributions to make that will enhance the goal or the way in which it is achieved.

As we know, effective communication means listening more than talking, so introducing a mentoring culture into your organization can improve communication because mentoring is essentially a dialogue between two people, with the mentor listening as much as talking. Mentors don't have to be managers; experienced staff members have a lot to offer new employees.

## KNOCK DOWN THE BARRICADES

Obstructions may crop up in many different guises. Common ones are fear, limiting or hindering beliefs, lack of self-confidence, anger and frustration. This is where mentoring can really help. Belief is often a principle or conviction that is accepted as true and is no longer questioned. As a mentor who is an effective communicator, it's your job to challenge any obstructions. Your role allows you to ask probing questions to challenge limiting beliefs. Encourage staff members to explore beliefs and perceptions, help them evaluate their thinking, and promote change in their perceptions and attitudes. Support them when they have to leave their comfort zones.

To do this, you need to ask your employee or colleague certain questions:

- Where did this belief come from?
- Who gave you this belief?
- What is this belief costing you on a daily basis?
- What will holding on to this belief mean for you in the long term if you don't do something about it?
- How will your life be different if you let go of this belief?

A good manager or mentor can achieve a paradigm shift by making his employee or colleague aware of their belief and its origins and by giving them the tools needed to move forward.

## BUILD UP YOUR COMMON BONDS

Any environment where an individual believes that their opinion is considered and valued, where they enjoy good relationships with their colleagues and bosses, will be a happy and productive environment. Contemporaries will often form friendships – relationships that only exist within the workplace but that are based on shared experiences and ideas. It's vital that these do not have a common base in the resentment of senior levels. To this end, a manager needs to build rapport with employees just as employees build rapport with each other. It sounds obvious, but effective communication is the answer! This may mean introducing specific times for talking and coaxing ideas from everyone, including less confident employees People who don't take credit for what they do, or are constantly apologizing, may appear weaker and less confident than they actually are.

I once interviewed the manager of a vessel manufacturing company that had introduced a suggestion session every week. One engineer put forward a recommendation to insert rivets every 46 instead of every 31 centimetres in the vessel they were building. Previously he wouldn't have said anything for fear of it not being important enough to warrant a mention, but because of the specific time put aside every week for ideas, however big or small, he was empowered to speak up. His suggestion eventually saved the company hundreds of thousands of pounds.

To put in a mentoring culture, you need to ask the more experienced employees to give the benefit of their knowledge to help newer or less skilled members of the workforce. The mentee needs to be confident that the mentor is reliable and will respect confidences.

As a mentor, your focus needs to be on the individual, you need to listen without evaluating and give advice when asked. Empathy is essential; you have to be able to understand and respect the feelings, opinions and drive of the other person in order to help them achieve empowerment and give them the confidence to be more self-reliant and responsible for their own decisions and actions. Although your role is largely to listen, it's helpful to be able to identify with your mentee, recollecting similar experiences from your past. This reassures them that you have travelled their journey and have faced the same challenges and insecurities.

### Putting it all together

To communicate effectively in the workplace, you need to have an open and empathetic culture that encourages discussion, innovation and self-development. Time should be set aside to encourage ideas and plans. A mentor should:

- ask probing questions and then summarize and paraphrase what has been said
- keep the questions focused and allow pauses to allow the other person time to think carefully before they answer
- recapitulate what has been said to make sure they have understood.

You need to prove that you have listened, heard and understood. As a mentor, you can encourage, direct, remedy and reassure your mentee. As a mentee, you should expect your mentor's full attention and comprehensive guidance, while remembering that they are not counsellors or Samaritans.

When tackling disciplinary issues with members of staff, it is vital to be tactful and polite, but the message must get through. Take the scenario of having to tell a salesman that late appointments are starting to lose business for the firm. 'Jim, I want to talk to you about Walker Bros. It seems you have been late for the last three appointments. It would be a pity to spoil such a good sales record, wouldn't it? So I'm sure it won't happen again.' Said with a smile, this takes the sting out of the rebuke without losing authority.

# 34 Make your meetings productive

*'For any meeting, keep the focus positive as much as you can. If negative issues must come up, focus only on negatives that affect the entire organization, rather than singling out individuals or departments.'* Matt Krumrie, business consultant

*'If you had to identify in one word, the reason why the human race has not achieved, and never will achieve, its full potential, that word would be "meetings".'* Dave Barry

*'Meetings are indispensable when you don't want to do anything.'* J. K. Galbraith

*'I just hate meetings.'* J. K. Rowling

*'When I have meetings scheduled so tight I can't go to the loo, that's when I draw the line!'* Christian Louboutin

Meetings are a fact of life in the business world but sometimes it is difficult to get your point across if you aren't very confident. To make the most of meetings, it is essential to be prepared and to realize that you would not be asked to attend if you didn't have something useful to communicate. Badly managed meetings waste time and can have a negative effect on company morale if people feel they are taken away from their desks for no good reason. Time is an important asset in business so, if meetings are unproductive, the company's bottom line will suffer: time is money.

9 10 11 12 13 14 15 16 17 18 19 20 21 22 23 24 25 26 27 28 29 30 31 32 33 34 35 36 37 38 39 40 41 42 43 44 45 46 47 48 49 50

When you arrange a meeting, begin with the end in mind; what is it you want the meeting to achieve? When arranging to see a client, always ask how much time that person has for a meeting and clarify expectations to make sure you understand what they are expecting. The role of the chairperson or moderator is vital, as he or she is there to control the meeting. Notes or minutes should be distributed as soon as possible. If other important topics are brought up, fix a time to talk about them or arrange another meeting if the situation is urgent. If possible, don't introduce any extra matter, as it will make everything and everybody run late.

**Furthermore**

As with most things in life, preparation is vital and is the key to successful meetings, so appoint the right chairperson. Once the agenda is written and circulated, make sure meetings have a start and end time so that people can plan their day. Be realistic and don't try to fit in too much and organize visual aids and handouts if needed.

Weekly meetings will help keep staff abreast of different projects as well as the state of the company or organization on a regular basis, but for many companies once or twice a month will do. Most people don't like last-minute meetings as it disturbs their routine, so call one only if it is really necessary and give those attending as much warning as possible.

## HAVE YOUR SAY IN MEETINGS

If you feel you may be intimidated by others after speaking up in a meeting, make your point early as this will give you confidence as well as make your presence felt. Shaking your head or even tut-tutting will show others that you disagree with what is being said. If this goes unnoticed, then you have to interject, but never lose your temper: losing your temper will also lose you the argument and your credibility.

**If you feel yourself getting heated, take some deep breaths and hold them for a count of three. This will help lower your blood pressure and clear your mind.**

## FILL THE CHAIR AND CONTROL THE MEETING

If you are chairing a meeting, you must insist that questions and comments 'go through the Chair' in order to keep the meeting disciplined. If everyone starts talking at the same time, chaos will reign! Start on time and don't wait for latecomers. Keep things to the point and stay focused on the reason for the meeting. Allow everyone to have their say but be strict about time. Take notes or minutes and circulate them as soon as possible after the meeting.

**It is important to praise people when something is well done. Nodding your head, smiling and verbally agreeing also shows approval for good ideas and strategies.**

If you are a participant, be prepared by making notes beforehand to ensure that you remember questions or points and can interject when necessary. To create a positive impression, aim to sit straight and don't straddle a chair or sit with arms behind your head. Obviously, the more familiar you are with the people and the circumstances, the more your posture can relax.

Unless you are expecting an urgent call, try to keep all phones switched off at meetings (see Secret 13). If the phone does ring, tell the caller politely that you will ring them back. Make the call as brief as possible, and either leave the room, or gesture to the client that you won't be long.

## SIT IN THE POSITION THAT SUITS THE SUBJECT

Where you sit or stand in a meeting can have an influential effect on the outcome. This is because people receive different types of information in different ways. For most people, the emotional side of our nature comes from the right hemisphere of the brain and the more logical side comes from the left – but the data is received the other way round.

- If you stand or sit to the *left* of your 'audience', you will be talking to their right brain and this is good if your subject is more abstract.
- For facts and figures, it is best to target the left side of the brain, so you would make your presentation standing or sitting to the *right* of your audience.

- Tests have shown that people who sit at the front usually learn and retain more than those sitting either at the back or the sides of a room so, if you are running an event, a horseshoe shape is the best, in order to engage everybody.

Most people don't like to sit with their back to an open door or space, as it can make them feel vulnerable. For a friendly meeting or chat, the best position is to sit diagonally across a table if you can. If you want to encourage trust, sit next to someone, as it is less confrontational. If you want to negotiate a deal, it is best not to sit opposite them as this can encourage competitive feelings – again, a diagonal position is best.

It is important to look alert, so sitting up straight and leaning slightly forward show you are interested and listening intently. Take a look round the room; how are others reacting to what is being said? You might lose interest because the topic is not relevant to you but, if everybody else is absorbed, listen carefully because you could be missing something crucial. If, however, you feel somebody is taking too long to make a point, leaning back in your chair and looking at your notes should give the speaker signals that you have lost interest in what he or she is saying.

**The way you sit is critical: to look and feel confident, look alert, sit straight, keep your head up and make eye contact with everyone.**

## Putting it all together

If you are running a meeting, prepare properly and make sure that only the relevant people are invited so that nobody's time is wasted. Name the time and the place and send an agenda and make certain you stick to it.

Sit upright but relaxed and lean forward when saying your piece. A smile will encourage people to listen to you, as well as warming your voice. It will also make you look confident and in control.

Reading body language is essential to make sure everybody is given equal time to air their views. Someone sitting forward in their chair or leaning on a desk is much more likely to be listening with interest to what you have to say. If someone is unhappy, they will move back and sit against the back of the chair, or lean against a wall if standing. They will turn their head away and often put a hand to their mouth as if to stifle a response – or possibly a yawn. They could drum their fingers or fiddle with a watch or jewellery or roll their head to free built-up tension in the neck or purse their lips. All this shows that there is opposition or even annoyance at what is being said, so the subject should be changed as soon as possible.

The way people use their hands in meetings is also important. 'Steepling' – that is, putting the forefingers or all the fingers together rather like a church steeple – can show concentration and empathy. Glasses often have a role to play in this context: some people gain thinking time by polishing their glasses or slowly and deliberately folding them before answering a question.

# 35 Take and make effective conference calls

*'I wake up every morning and I feel like I'm juggling glass balls. I live in Los Angeles, my business is run out of London, and most evenings I'm cuddled up in front of Skype, in my dressing gown, speaking with my studio in London. I travel a lot, my team travel a lot, but I wouldn't have it any other way.'*
Victoria Beckham

*'Skype is for any individual who has a broadband Internet connection.'* Niklas Zennstrom

*'I don't care how someone lives or how good their spoken English is. I do all of my interviews on Skype text chat – all that matters is their work.'* Matt Mullenweg

*'I don't even have voicemail or answering machines anymore. I hate the phone, and I don't want to call anybody back. If I go to hell, it will be a small closet with a telephone in it, and I will be doomed and destined for eternity to return phone calls.'*
Drew Barrymore

*'The night before, go over your schedule and see what you're going to do and what the purpose of what you're doing is. I advocate having a two-column schedule. On the left, put down all your appointments and phone calls. On the right, put down what the purpose is.'* Robert Pozen

Conference calls are used for job interviews and media calls as well as for meetings between organizations and between colleagues and clients. The most important thing for any conference call, as for any meeting, is to have an agenda and a moderator or chairperson to lead the call; otherwise it can become a free-for-all. If you are a participant, write down any questions you want to raise because it is easy to get sidetracked.

If you want to come across as a confident communicator, it is vital to use your voice and your body positively. Vivacity and enthusiasm must show in your voice if it is an audio conference call, and you must appear assured, alert and competent for a video call. Since most of us have no idea how we sound on the phone, it is useful to record yourself making a phone call, playing it back and analysing it. Like the first visual impression, the first vocal one is important and it can be decisive when it is part of an interview or a sales call. For the same reason, it is beneficial to practise chatting in front of the camera. Talk to an imaginary client or colleague to iron out any subconscious gestures or inhibitions so that you can become confident and in control of the medium. Video yourself listening to friends or family, to make sure you have active listening skills.

Internal conference calls are a useful way of keeping employees motivated, especially for people working from home. It can keep everyone in touch and on message as well as disseminating information and company news. But, like meetings, they should only be employed when there is a good reason. A weekly call that achieves nothing and only wastes time will be resented and become counterproductive after a while.

**Furthermore**

Video and Skype calls can save a huge amount of stress and money in time and travel. Although it is always better to meet clients and customers face to face if possible, it is quite feasible to build a good relationship over the ether if you can come across as natural and confident. This means speaking clearly and concisely, listening energetically and being thoroughly prepared.

## LISTEN WITH THE RIGHT EAR

To listen attentively, it makes a surprising difference which ear you listen with. You tend to listen with the right ear when you are absorbing complicated information because it connects with the logical half of the brain, which is the left side. You use your left ear when listening empathetically, as it connects with the more creative, right side of the brain. All this happens subconsciously, but tests have shown that, if you hold a receiver to the left ear when listening to a friend's problems, it helps you concentrate better. Equally, if you are listening to directions, you are more likely to remember them if you listen with your right ear.

When dealing with complaints, keep calm and try to work out the nature of the complaint before deciding which ear to use. If the callers' tone of voice is anxious, you will need to allow them to voice all their complaints without interruption, so listen sympathetically with your left ear. Wait until they have finished and then take them through the complaints step by step. This shows them that you have taken note of what they have said, which goes a long way towards appeasing anger or frustration. If the complainant's tone is strident and belligerent, try not to lose your temper and avoid matching your vocal tone to theirs. If they shout and raise their voice and you do the same, it will only exacerbate the problem, so tell them politely and calmly that you cannot do anything to help until you have taken the full details of their complaint. Get their name and take them back to the beginning, going through their grievances one by one.

## TALK THE TALK IN PHONE INTERVIEWS

Some organizations employ companies to sift through applicants by conducting the first interview over the phone, so the way you come across is vital. There are several things to be aware of, over-familiarity being one; allow the interviewer to take the lead. Beware of giving yes and no answers because they will not give the interviewer any idea of your personality and originality. Ask questions; this is essential for you to find out more about the organization as well as allowing the interviewer to gauge your character by the questions you ask. Take notes, if not during the call, as soon as you put the phone down so that you can recollect and evaluate the call properly.

**Remember how smiling when using the phone helps to 'warm' the voice.**

When being interviewed by a radio or press journalist, it is essential to clear your desk so that you are not distracted by anything. Listening intently is imperative, especially with a press reporter, as you don't know how much of the story they have already written, so have questions ready to try to ascertain how much they know or whether they are just 'fishing'. If you are caught on the hop or feel unprepared, you can 'stall but call' – calling back after checking any relevant facts and information. Give yourself time to think.

It is also crucial to have a clear mind for any conference call so that you can listen to the nuances of what is being said. If there are a number of people on the call, you cannot be sure if someone isn't contributing because they have nothing to add, or whether they have gone to empty the bins or make a cup of coffee! When chairing or moderating a call, make sure you talk to everyone and ask individuals frequent questions to keep them alert and on board.

## WATCH HOW YOU LOOK AND WHAT YOU WEAR

For a video conference call, how you look and what you wear are important factors. Make sure your location and your clothes are appropriate for the occasion. If you have a certain image to maintain in the workplace, don't appear in your most casual clothes because you are working from home.

It is important to look into the camera so that you can establish eye contact as much as possible. To get the most out of the call, it is essential to lean forward when listening and to nod or shake your head to show whether you agree or not with what is being said. Make sure you don't move too much as Skype and some video links can still be unreliable at times; over-the-top gestures and erratic body language can be distracting, so keep the hands away from your face, don't fiddle with pens or papers and don't have a surreptitious cup of tea – you must show that your concentration is focused on what is being discussed.

## Putting it all together

Listen to a conference call with your full attention, and smile when you speak to 'warm' your voice. Bear in mind that we listen with the right ear when we are absorbing complex information because it connects with the logical left half of the brain, whereas we use our left ear when listening empathetically as it connects with the more artistic right side of the brain.

Have any necessary notes near the phone, but make sure that the rest of the desk or table is clear. It is easy to be distracted and you need to concentrate harder when there is nobody to look at. Be brief but factual when you talk, and listen for changes in voices to help you pick up the nuances of what is being discussed. If you are being told about a concept, product or service, it helps to concentrate on whoever is talking so you don't lose focus; vital opportunities can be missed if you don't give a call your full attention. If a call is likely to be difficult, take the initiative and get quickly to the point.

For a video conference, choose your location carefully because your surroundings will be noted. Practise active listening, looking into the camera to establish eye contact. If you are trying to understand a tricky problem or a complicated scenario, repeat the main points to make sure you have understood correctly. Lastly, never forget that you are the image of your company or organization at all times.

# 36 Understand why the customer is always right

> *'There is only one boss. The customer. And he can fire everybody in the company from the chairman on down, simply by spending his money somewhere else.'* Sam Walton

> *'A man without a smiling face must not open a shop.'* Chinese proverb

> *'The best way to find yourself is to lose yourself in the service of others.'* Mahatma Ghandi

> *'To understand the man, you must first walk a mile in his moccasins.'* Native American proverb

> *'Courteous treatment will make a customer a walking advertisement.'* J. C. Penney

> *'Nothing is so contagious as enthusiasm.'* Samuel Taylor Coleridge

In truth, the customer is not always right – no one working in a service industry should have to put up with abusive or insulting behaviour when they are helping others. Nor should they be cheated or tricked by dishonest customers. It can be difficult to deal with people who are demanding, selfish and irrational but this is a skill you need if you work in this sector.

Customers who are honest and reasonable have the right to expect good, courteous service. If you are employed in this sector, you need a good understanding of common courtesy and to be able to show genuine consideration for others. You



9 10 11 12 13 14 15 16 17 18 19 20 21 22 23 24 25 26 27 28 29 30 31 32 33 34 35 36 37 38 39 40 41 42 43 44 45 46 47 48 49 50

also have to work with many different individuals, often from different countries with different cultures. It is important that you demonstrate the highest level of politeness and respect to everyone you deal with, not only customers but also your co-workers: teamwork is essential to make customer service work, and one rude member of staff can ruin the reputation of a whole organization.

To succeed in this industry, you have to be confident enough in your social skills to establish appropriate, professional relationships with your customers and staff and know the correct etiquette when speaking to customers, using their appropriate title and name. It goes without saying that you also need an excellent working knowledge of your products as well as of what cultural differences to expect on the global stage. Appearance, poise and interpersonal abilities are significant factors in building relationships with your customers. Although they can be infuriating and it can be hard to keep your temper, you must never show anger. You also have to learn how to cope with angry people, as well as handling bullies, intolerance and prejudice. You need to be able to communicate with confidence to handle this kaleidoscope of human behaviour! It is important to anticipate customer needs and be aware of possible problems, therefore helping to avoid them. Speaking with clarity and authority is also vital when transmitting confidence and a positive image.

## PUT YOURSELF IN YOUR CUSTOMERS' SHOES

If you work in the hospitality sector, it is imperative to provide a sincere welcome to make your clientele feel valued. That is what makes the difference when people recommend hotels, bars, cafés or restaurants – even more than price. Eye contact is essential here, as is posture, but attitude is the key thing.

You need to put yourself in the customers' shoes and anticipate their requirements. If the weather is bad and they have had to struggle through snow, for instance, they might be a bit tetchy, so take that into account and show some sympathy, especially if they arrive late. The way you use your voice can do a lot to calm people and avoid stress for both you and your guests.

When dealing with complaints from guests, use the same techniques as those described in Secret 37 for making your own complaints. Keep calm, allow them to voice their complaints without interruption and then take them through your solution step by step. Eye contact, nodding and active listening will do much to diffuse tricky situations, but it is important to make sure that the complaint is acted upon and the problem solved if possible.

- If you are dealing with several customers at once at the bar, make eye contact and smile and nod at those who are waiting so that they know they are in your radar.
- When you are waiting, look alert. It looks smart to stand with arms behind your back.
- If you are in business, never ask a customer or client to ring back. If they have taken the trouble to contact you, you or your boss should return the call.

## MAKE THE CUSTOMER FEEL SPECIAL

Working in a service industry necessitates long hours, aching feet and a calm disposition. As with any occupation, it is important to leave your troubles at home so that you can concentrate on the people you are serving, as well as those you are working with. The retail trade is under a lot of pressure because many businesses are now selling goods online, which means that shops need fewer staff. In your customer service role it is up to you to make sure shoppers feel special, so that they won't just browse the Internet, they will come into your store. Make sure that you give shoppers the best experience you possibly can.

Sam Walton is right: there is only one boss and that is the customer. While there is obviously the pressure to sell clothes and accessories, strive to be as honest and tactful as you can. There is no need to tell a customer that she looks awful in the outfit she is struggling to get into but, if a dress really doesn't suit her, instead of telling her she looks fabulous when she obviously doesn't, offer some alternatives that you think will fit and encourage her to try those.

Get to know your merchandise as well as you know yourself. You cannot sell anything unless you understand what you are talking about. For example, if you work in a clothes store, your knowledge of comparable sizes from different labels and the 'in' colours and fabrics should all be second nature. It is a matter of keeping up to date and doing your research. If you get a name for honest and sound advice, your reputation will spread far and wide.

## BE A SUCCESS IN CUSTOMER CARE

To make a career in customer service, you have to enjoy working with people. This is known as 'customer care' because, if you don't care for your customers, you will fail in this industry. If you aren't interested in understanding people and their likes and dislikes, then you really should be looking for another job. Creating the right image for any establishment is important. If you are seen slouching against a wall or chatting to colleagues instead of attending to customers, the status of your organization is likely to suffer, so be aware that you are always 'on show'.

Again, although it is important to be on friendly terms with customers, don't overdo the conversation. If you work as a hairdresser or in a spa, for instance, read the body talk. If the reply to your enquiry is a one-word answer, it will usually mean that the person is preoccupied and doesn't want to talk. If you do ask questions, listen properly to the answers – don't just go through the motions. It is annoying for a client, after answering the 'Where are you going on holiday?' question, to be asked again two minutes later.

Controlling your temper is crucial in any service industry. Who or what pushes your anger buttons? If you know what might make you angry, it is easier to avoid it and keep anger under control.

**Remember the importance of smiling: if you are glum and disgruntled when serving customers, what should be a pleasurable experience for them turns into anything but.**

## Putting it all together

To earn respect from customers and co-workers, you have to value what you do so that you will do it to the best of your ability. It is important to establish and maintain professional relationships with customers and your colleagues. It is also essential to feel comfortable in an environment with different cultures, languages and ethnic backgrounds.

To be able to carry out your duties competently and with an air of confidence, elegance, sophistication and – above all – professionalism, the way you dress is crucial. If you wear a uniform, it should fit and be maintained properly, including the shoes. Hair should be neat and off the face for hygiene purposes in many sectors, as well as for a professional look.

You have to know what to do when things go wrong and manage difficult and delicate situations with diplomacy and tact, as well as showing respect and support for your colleagues, so it is crucial to be able to work as a team. To provide a sincere welcome, it helps to remember the importance of:

- smiling and making eye contact
- maintaining a posture that shows attentiveness
- reading body language to help you understand the customer's requirements
- putting yourself in your customers' shoes so that you can anticipate their wishes.

These actions also help when dealing with complaints from customers or staff. If a customer starts shouting, keep your voice even to take the heat out of the situation. The use of the voice and the expression on your face all help to build rapport. And never underestimate the importance of a smile!

# 37 Make effective complaints with confidence

> *'Your most unhappy customers are your greatest source of learning.'* Bill Gates

> *'In the end, the customer doesn't know, or care, if you are small or large as an organization. She or he only focuses on the garment hanging on the rail in the store.'* Giorgio Armani

> *'Customers don't expect you to be perfect. They do expect you to fix things when they go wrong.'* Donald Porter, VP, British Airways

> *'In the world of Internet Customer Service, it's important to remember your competitor is only one mouse click away.'* Doug Warner

> *'The most important adage and the only adage is, the customer comes first; whatever the business, the customer comes first.'* Kerry Stokes

Despite all the training that goes into customer service, the quotes above are only relevant to the thinking of about half the organizations you are likely to deal with. However, most businesses would say they have a customer service policy, so bear this in mind when you make a complaint and analyse the quotes above.

Many small businesses cannot afford expensive training and rely on their staff to follow the example of the manager or business owner. Some organizations still don't believe that customer service training is particularly important. Despite the emphasis on quality and customer care, there are still many places where standards are not high, especially where the staff are young and wages are low.

If you have a valid grievance, you have every right to protest, so have the self-confidence to make a complaint. However, if you are going to communicate your displeasure, make sure you do it politely. If the service isn't good, don't leave a tip. It is important to say when you are not pleased with the way you have been treated, but you will get much further if you are courteous and well mannered. Things go wrong in every industry, but most of us don't bother to complain because we lack the confidence, feel embarrassed or don't think it will do any good.

## REMEMBER BLAST!

BLAST is not a curse; B.L.A.S.T is part of many retailers' customer service training. If you work in a customer-facing situation, this is a good acronym to remember; if you are a customer making a complaint, it helps to know that many people are trained in this way.

- B is for Believing the customer has a grievance.
- L is for Listening to the complaint .
- A is for Acting on what you have heard.
- S is for Service to make sure things are put right in the future.
- T is for Thank you for being told what went wrong.

If you are complaining, decide first what you want to achieve. Do you want a refund, a repair, an apology or replacement of goods? Remain courteous at all times and never lose your temper. All companies should look at complaints as feedback: if customers don't complain if a product or service is not up to scratch, customer service will not improve.

## NEVER MAKE A SCENE

We all have grievances at some time, so how do we deal with them? It is all too easy to lose one's temper but it is important to try to avoid making a scene at all costs. Showing anger may relieve your stress in the short term but it will probably mean you won't be able to go back to that establishment again and you never know who else may have been observing you blow your top!

If you are in a restaurant, call the waiter to one side and stand or sit up straight and keep your voice even. Look the person in the eye and smile. Then tell him or her quietly and calmly what is wrong and ask them what they are going to do about it. For example, if a waiter or waitress asks you if everything is all right and it patently isn't, say so: 'We ordered some drinks a while ago now. Are they on their way?' It is important to speak to the person in charge if you have a serious complaint because the buck stops with them.

**Furthermore**

Doctors are also increasingly under pressure from patients waiting for treatment. If you want to complain to your doctor about something, always gather the information you need and have it in front of you when making the complaint. It is a good idea to make notes after telephone calls so that the facts stay in your mind. Then go through your points one by one in a calm and composed manner. Be firm about what you expect and, if possible, get a date for your operation or consultation before you finish the conversation.

## PRACTISE MAKING A COMPLAINT BEFORE YOU MAKE IT

Take the following steps when you practise making a complaint:

1. Write down the facts of your complaint, whether it is real or imaginary.
2. Record yourself making the complaint. The tone of your voice is vital, so listen back and analyse the conversation.
3. Practise your body language: try to avoid crossing your arms in a barrier position as it can alienate your listener; they may feel you have already made up your mind and are not prepared to listen to their side of the story.

If you are planning to complain face to face, remember that understanding the other person's body talk can help you know how to respond. If someone steeples their hands, it usually means they are listening and analysing what you are saying. If they are trying to remember something, they will glance to the left, whereas when creating thoughts or telling untruths, they are more likely to look to the right.

## Putting it all together

It is important not to become a serial complainer. Some people make it a habit and almost part of their lifestyle. I heard of a woman who bought a suit from an Internet company and sent it back after 28 days, saying it was the wrong colour. She got different coloured suits for the next six months until the company got suspicious and stopped sending any more garments.

A courteous complaint will not antagonize and will allow you to keep control, thus allowing you to be seen as reasonable and to get the best results or compensation. Keep these two points in mind:

- Be clear about what you expect and firm about what you will accept.
- Be civil, and you will find that disputes are settled more quickly and agreeably.

If you raise your voice, your adversary (and it does become adversarial) will raise theirs and the situation can soon become a slanging match – if not an outbreak of fisticuffs! It is important to say when you are not pleased with the way you have been treated, but you will get much further if you are well mannered.

# 38 Find out what it takes to kick-start your career

*'Some people don't understand the importance of presentation in a job interview. If you want to be certain NOT to get a job, come to the interview dressed how you feel that day. Show up late, shake hands like your arm went numb, talk endlessly, chew gum, bring a friend, make fun of your last employer, and only ask questions about holidays and staff parties. For added certainty, mention this quote from the film* Double Indemnity*: "There is a widespread feeling that just because a man has a large office he must be an idiot."'*

(Taken from *Reel Life Wisdom – The Worst Movie Quotes for an Interview*)

*'Luck is what happens when preparation meets opportunity.'*
Seneca

*'Choose a job you love, and you will never have to work a day in your life.'* Confucius

*'Whenever you are asked if you can do a job, tell 'em, "Certainly I can!" Then get busy and find out how to do it.'* Theodore Roosevelt

*'Take time to deliberate; but when the time for action arrives, stop thinking and go in.'* Napoleon Bonaparte

When applying for a job, preparation is all: it is the key to confidence and confidence is the key to success. The crucial thing is to find out as much as you can about the company you want to work for. Don't ask, as one interviewee did when applying for a job at one of the Fortune 500 companies, 'What is it that you people do at this company?' He didn't get the chance to ask a second question!

Interviewing techniques vary from company to company. You could be interviewed one to one or by a panel or board. Both of these have advantages and disadvantages. Find out who the interviewer is, what part they play in the recruitment process and how long the interview is likely to take.

A good interviewer should:

- start the interview on time
- have your details on the desk in front of them
- ask open questions, allowing you to expand to include the points you want to get across.

There is also the 'halo and horns' syndrome to be taken into account. We tend to warm to people who share our own values and views, but good interviewers will be aware of this and disregard it as much as possible. Some interviewers take notes, but don't be anxious if they don't: it doesn't mean that you are so boring there is nothing to write about! Your task is to convince a prospective employer that you can do the job and that you are interested in their industry. It is a waste of their time to train you for six months, only to find that you don't like the job after all and decide to leave.

If the people conducting the interview are not properly trained, it can be an uncomfortable experience. The thing to remember in such interviews is that it is not personal, so keep your cool. The interview may well be running late, and the interviewer can do all the talking, not allowing you to get your carefully prepared points across. If that interviewer is the type of person who makes snap decisions and you don't get the job, don't lose heart; put it down to experience!

**For any interview, it is essential 'to walk in like a winner' and put across a positive image.**

## KNOW HOW TO DEAL WITH DIFFERENT TYPES OF QUESTION

A sign of untrained or inexperienced interviewers is that they will probably ask closed or leading questions in a rather haphazard way, frequently interrupting. For example: 'Do you think you could do the job? I mean… you have got the right qualifications, haven't you?' (searching frantically for your CV). 'Which company was it you worked for?' Before an interview, think of the points you want to get across and make a note of them. This will help you to make sure that you cover everything you want to cover, even if the interviewer seems to be unsure of what questions to ask. When your mind goes blank, headings will help to jog the memory. Think of some questions you may want to ask and make a note of them too. Don't feel you have to ask questions at the end: it's fine to say, 'Thank you very much, but I think you've covered everything I need to know.'

**Closed questions** have a specific answer:

- Did you…
- Who was…
- Which company…

**Leading questions** can look for opinion or comment:

- Do you think you…
- Can you…
- Are you…

**Open questions** require information from you:

- Why did you…
- When were you…
- Where have you…
- How did you…

**Hypothetical questions** are designed to make you think:

- What would you do if…
- How would you tackle…
- Supposing that…

**Furthermore**

Taking notes during an interview also impresses many prospective employers because it indicates that you are showing real interest. Don't just use a cheap ballpoint; have a nice pen and a folder or book for taking notes.

## GIVE THE ANSWERS YOU WANT TO GIVE

Before an interview, make a note of any evidence of how you have done specific things that are asked for in the job spec. Obviously, being asked open questions is ideal but, if you think you are being interviewed by somebody who isn't bringing out the best in you, answer a closed or leading question as if it were an open one. If asked, 'Do you think you have initiative?' instead of just answering 'Yes', you might say, 'I do think I have initiative because last year, when we had a small fire in the office, people started to panic so I sounded the alarm, told someone to ring the fire brigade and then made sure everyone was evacuated quickly and quietly.' With the question, 'Are you willing to travel with this job?' your answer could be, 'Yes. I have travelled a lot ever since I left school and always enjoyed the challenge of meeting new people and seeing new places.' Try to answer these questions as honestly as you can and imagine what the ideal employee would do, taking into account the job description.

## KNOW WHAT QUESTIONS TO EXPECT

You can never know exactly what questions you will be asked at an interview, but the following table shows some examples, the reasons for them and possible answers.

All the answers given tell the interviewer something positive about you. Whatever you do as a hobby, try to relate it to the job you are going for. If the job on offer means plenty of foreign travel and your hobby is cooking, that answer would tell the prospective employer that you would probably feel at home entertaining clients in different countries. If a job demanded teamwork and resourcefulness, the fact that you play in teams and work on your own to find sponsorship proves you can use your initiative but also work well with others.

| Question | Reason for question | Possible answer |
|---|---|---|
| **What have you learned from your last job?** | This is asking you to summarize the skills and knowledge you have gained. | As senior sales assistant, I had to deal with all kinds of queries, from staff as well as customers. I also had to make sure the goods were displayed properly, handle the accounts and, most useful of all, learn to negotiate with suppliers. |
| **What would you consider as adequate reward for your efforts?** | This sort of question is to test you and learn more about your personality. If you have already found out what the salary is, quote the figure mentioned. | I would naturally like to be paid the going rate for my services! But more than that, I would want the chance to develop my skills as a manager and expand my knowledge of the industry. |
| **What are your hobbies?** | This question is usually asked to find out more about you and your physical and mental health. | I like cooking. It helps me relax and I love finding new recipes in different countries when I travel.<br><br>*or*<br><br>I play football in the winter and cricket in the summer. I enjoy being part of a team. I also organize sponsorship for both teams to help fund travel and new equipment. |

## Putting it all together

Research shows that most interview decisions are made within the first 60 seconds, often before the candidate has even opened his or her mouth! How you walk, how you say 'Hello' and how you are dressed all go to form a positive or negative image. There are several things interviewers for any position will look out for: first impressions, relevant experience and necessary skills as well as your reason for applying.

You should know what the organization does, who owns it, the key personnel and how many people it employs. It also helps to know its reputation and whether the annual turnover is increasing or decreasing. It sounds obvious, but know the job title of the job you are going for. It is also a good idea to ask about terms and conditions and the way the job will develop.

Interviewers should shake hands before you sit down, but if they don't, make sure you shake their hands at the end of the interview, as they might be waiting to see if you are confident enough to take the initiative. A good, positive handshake is vital.

Eye contact is also important because you cannot tell what someone thinks or means unless you look into their eyes. Respond to a question by looking at whoever asked it, even if that person is busy writing notes. Listening skills are essential, too; an interview can be thrown off course if you answer the question you thought you heard rather than the one that was asked.

1 2 3 4 5 6 7 8 9 10 11 12 13 14 15 16 17 18 19 20 21 22 23 24 25 26 27 28 29 30 31 32 33 34 35 36 37 38 39 40 41 42 43 44 45 46 47 48 49 50

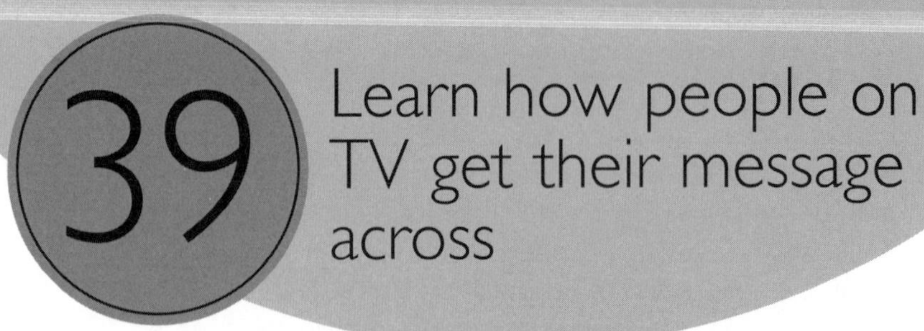

# 39 Learn how people on TV get their message across

*'Over the years, during television interviews, whenever the host or the reviewer or whoever gets cynical and nasty with me, I will behave accordingly. I will defend myself.'* John Lydon

*'I sometimes find that in interviews you learn more about yourself than the person learned about you.'* William Shatner

*'You know, there's that temptation in interviews to make yourself sound – well, to give yourself a bit of mystery.'* Johnny Vegas

*'I am always asking myself why is this lying **** lying to me?'* Jeremy Paxman

*'I am really bad at actually interviewing people.'* Graham Norton

*'Confidence has a lot to do with interviewing – that, and timing.'* Michael Parkinson

You can learn a lot about communication from watching good television presenters. They don't have long to get their message across, so they learn to condense an opinion, an idea or an argument into a short space of time. This takes skill and experience but, if you can develop the talent, it can be extremely useful at meetings or in business negotiations. Television is also a brilliant way to spread a message. So how do you become a confident communicator on TV?

The first thing is to know your subject and then practise talking about it. As I have said in previous secrets, recording yourself is an excellent way of clarifying your thoughts. All TV interviews have to run to a given time, so practising getting your message across in 30 seconds, 1 minute or 5 minutes is incredibly good training for any kind of communication. If you decide to make TV part of your marketing mix, you need to watch the type of programmes that might suit your product, service or cause. Look at them critically and see where you might fit in. Look at the reporters and presenters and learn their style of questioning.

When you think that TV commercials can cost thousands of pounds to make, if you can get yourself on TV for free it is worth getting it right. You never know just how much your interviewer knows about your subject, but they or their researchers will have dug up the key facts so they will have a clear idea of the questions they are going to ask. You will not be told in advance those exact questions, but you should be given an idea of the areas liable to be covered. It is a good idea to ask what the first question is going to be, as this will give you an inkling of the tack they are likely to take.

'Seek first to understand then to be understood' is a good maxim. If you can understand people's motivation, experience, needs and values, you can construct answers that will give the presenter and your audience what they want.

## GRAB THE VIEWER'S ATTENTION

TV is now a part of everyday life that we take completely for granted. Many viewers are doing other things while watching TV: preparing a meal, doing the ironing, reading the paper or using other technology, so you have to work quite hard to get them to watch you and take in what you are saying. This is where short, punchy sentences are key. You also have to appear animated and enthusiastic – if you don't look as though you care about what you are saying, why should the viewers?

TV companies are always looking for something new to fill their airtime. They will not do free advertising, however, so when you contact a specific programme or producer, you need to offer something of interest to that programme as well as to the local or national community.

As we have seen, to be confident when communicating you have to know how you come across to others. To find out whether you have what it takes to be a confident communicator on TV, you have to get to know your voice, your face and your body language. Body language is vital because, if viewers are only half watching, they will read your body talk even if they can't hear what you are saying.

All interviews should be one-to-one conversations unless you are in a group discussion. One comforting thing to remember for television interviews is that most people watch TV with probably no more than 70 per cent of their concentration. In many households the TV is on all the time, rather like moving wallpaper, so your problem is getting viewers to concentrate rather than worrying about them looking at every twitch or grimace.

## LOOK GOOD ON TV AND PROJECT THE IMAGE YOU WANT TO PROJECT

Think about the image you want to project. Darker colours are seen as more professional but bright colours will attract attention. Don't wear anything that will distract viewers from what you are saying: a very short skirt, large dangling earrings or trousers that show an expanse of flesh above your socks.

Since you will probably not be given make-up before you go on TV, it is a good idea – for both men and women – to powder their face, as a shiny face can look as though you are nervous, and high-definition cameras show up every line or blemish. It is important that you are happy with how you look. Make sure that you are well groomed, with tidy hair and clothes. Although people are only watching TV with roughly 70 per cent of their concentration, it is amazing what small details they do notice, hair being one of them. If you wear make-up, check that it is not smudged.

It is essential to look comfortable, but don't slouch – you want to look as though you have confidence and authority. If you are wearing a jacket, it is a good idea to sit on the tail so that your collar doesn't ride up. Hands should be relaxed, so clasp them lightly on your lap if you are sitting down for an interview. Legs can be crossed, but preferably at the ankles. Try to ignore the camera and concentrate on the interviewer and the questions being asked. It is very seldom that you will actually look into the camera lens unless you are doing a piece 'down the line', which means that you will be in a remote studio talking to a presenter via a link.

## COMMUNICATE YOUR MESSAGE WITH CONFIDENCE ON TV

Unless you are interviewed by someone like Jeremy Paxman, you shouldn't find you have a battle on your hands, but most good journalists will play the devil's advocate to give an interview more 'bite' and keep the viewers' interest. Once again, preparation is paramount, coupled with really knowing your subject. If you look at your topic from the viewer's point of view, this will give you a good pointer to the sort of questioning you are likely to meet. Make clear in advance any areas that you are not prepared to discuss. This is quite within your rights. There have been many cases of lack of liaison between producers and interviewers, resulting in questions being asked which the interviewee did not expect and is either unable or unwilling to answer. The resulting awkwardness can lead to unconvincing answers and a poor interview, which is not in anybody's best interests.

Look at different presenters and analyse why you think they are good communicators. Are their faces animated or do they have a passive expression when asking questions, for instance? Body language and communication skills are used differently in different circumstances. The broadcaster Fiona Bruce has to keep her voice and countenance neutral when she is reading the news, but she is much more animated when she is presenting *The Antiques Roadshow*. The gardening expert Monty Don's facial expressions and body language immediately tell us how much he loves his subject, even if we can't hear what he is saying. These people are chosen to work on TV not just because they are experts in their field but because they are also expert communicators and use their voices and their bodies to get their message across.

## Putting it all together

Simplicity and clarity are the lifeblood of a good interview. Decide the main point you wish to put over and make subsidiary points in descending order. This means that if the interview is cut short for whatever reason, only the less important points will go. Try to make the most important point again if possible, so that you can be sure it will hit home. Don't expect too much in terms of airtime. Although your particular topic is of the utmost importance to you, and hopefully to a wider audience as well, it has to fit into a busy programme schedule. Interviews typically last from two to three minutes.

When I started The Public Image Finishing School, I contacted our local BBC TV station and told them about the idea. They thought it would be of interest and came to film some of the classes. We got a lot of interest from the media and the public alike, and it really helped to grow the business. Although so many people now use the Internet rather than TV for news and entertainment and viewing figures have fallen since the growth of the net and easy downloads, there is still something magical about TV and it still has the power to publicize and promote ideas, inventions and products in a way that is accessible for all.

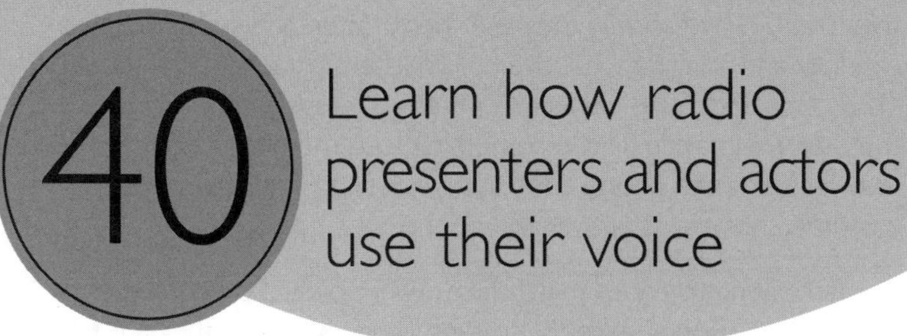

# 40 Learn how radio presenters and actors use their voice

*'The exhilarating ripple of her voice was a wild tonic in the rain.'*
**F. Scott Fitzgerald,** *The Great Gatsby*

*'I heard you on the wireless back in fifty-two,*
*Lying awake intent at tuning in on you.'* **Trevor Horn, 'Video Killed the Radio Star'**

*'There is no index of character so sure as the voice.'*
**Benjamin Disraeli**

*'The human voice is the organ of the soul.'* **Henry Wadsworth Longfellow**

*'I like doing radio because it's so intimate. The moment people hear your voice, you're inside their heads, not only that, you're in there laying eggs.'* **Douglas Coupland**

Communicating through the airways takes a particular skill, as you only have your voice to get your message across. When you listen to favourite presenters, try and analyse what it is you like about them. Is it their voice, their wit or their style? Most of us listen to the radio when we are driving or have it on when we are doing other things, so it is only the voice that will make listeners sit up and take notice. Analyse the voices on different programmes. How do different presenters use their voices? What is it about them that makes you tune in?

If you listen to drama on the radio, the actors have the power to transport us to a totally different world, not just by the words



9 10 11 12 13 14 15 16 17 18 19 20 21 22 23 24 25 26 27 28 29 30 31 32 33 34 35 36 37 38 39 40 41 42 43 44 45 46 47 48 49 50

they use but by the way they use them. Listen to various voices carefully and imagine what the broadcasters or actors look like. Very often, the voice paints an entirely different picture from the one we imagine. This is something to remember if your job involves using the phone a lot or if your first contact with your customers or clients is over the phone.

It is fascinating to try to match faces with voices. Some people have a 'deep brown' voice that makes listeners believe they are tall and dark when they might be totally the opposite. A woman with a high voice will sound younger than one with a deeper voice.

## LEARN FROM THE PILOTS OF THE AIRWAVES

The variety of radio programmes means that many different styles of presenter are required. Some stations expect their stars to talk more than others when presenting music, for instance, and if they are presenting talk shows, obviously they have to have the 'gift of the gab'. You can learn from each and every one of them.

It is not easy to think of something new and startling to say day after day on the radio, and there is a lot to think about when you are live on air. Managing the desk and possibly interviewing members of the public, politicians and various experts – in the studio, down the line or over the phone – require quick thinking. To be confident when constructing a good interview means listening carefully, reading body language and having a good level of general knowledge so that you can ask intelligent questions. Radio stations that purely play music need presenters with a quick mind, a good voice and the ability to get into the hearts and minds of the listeners. They need to make each one of us feel that they are talking to us individually, which is a great skill.

## KNOW HOW TO GIVE A GREAT RADIO INTERVIEW

Just as you would with a TV or press interview, begin your radio interview with the end in mind: what you want to get out of it. Always ask how long the interview is going to run and get an idea of the first question. Clarifying expectations and making sure you understand what the presenter is expecting from the interview will help you get your thoughts in order.

To ensure that you get across the points you want to make, you need to set the agenda as early as possible. This is not always easy, but using phrases like 'What you have to understand…' or 'To put things in context…' requires the interviewer to let you finish because the listeners will want answers to those statements. This allows you to get your main points in as early as possible so that they will be heard even if the interview is cut short.

Think win–win. What can the programme do for you and what can you do for the programme? To make an interview stimulating and relevant, you need to find ways to include all sections of your audience. To keep people's interest, the interview has to benefit them. Whether you are talking about your experiences, your work or your organization, you have to think of the wide spectrum of people listening. Put yourself in their shoes and try to understand what they need and want to hear. If you are talking about raising money for a charity, for instance, you have to put forward a convincing argument to your listeners to get them to part with their hard-earned cash. If you are giving an opinion as an expert, it means giving advice for all members of the audience, whatever their sex and age.

If you are taking part in an interview on the phone, at home or in the office, make sure you are in an environment that isn't distracting. The skills required are similar to those used in any business negotiation; the secret is to be able to remember and apply them in the totally different world of TV and radio. You will therefore need all your wits about you – this is a world in which your interviewer is completely at home and you are not. However, it is essential to remember that it is you who is the expert in your subject so don't let it appear otherwise.

Don't use notes unless you have to; if their use is unavoidable, refer to them openly and not furtively. Never arrive with a speech that is written out or previously learned; it simply will not work.

## UNDERSTAND THE ADVANTAGES OF RADIO OVER TV

Television had a huge impact on radio when it was a new medium, and for some time listening figures declined dramatically. People no longer sat around their radio sets listening avidly when they could cluster round the TV and watch images on the screen. Salaries in television were much higher than in radio and presenters rushed to work for the new medium. But the skills needed are subtly different and not everybody could make the transition.

Television is a visual medium and looks are very important; a melodious voice is not enough. It is not a matter of being handsome or beautiful, but 'televisual' – someone the camera likes and who likes the camera. Communication is sometimes easier on radio because it is an intimate medium. Often the 'hosts' are on their own in a small, cosy studio without lights and cameras, and this enables them to develop a very personal style. Studying and using this type of broadcasting style can be useful in some business negotiations.

## Putting it all together

Analyse what it is that makes a particular radio presenter a good communicator. Learn from how they use their voices, how they use words and how they make you feel. If you want to use radio to promote your product or service, be proactive. If you take the initiative and build rapport with your favoured presenter, you may find genuine common ground as well as opportunities for a stimulating discussion.

Listen to the programmes that could potentially offer you an opportunity for publicity. Most local radio stations need constant content and are always on the lookout for good communicators. They need experts to give interesting but impartial advice, so there is plenty of scope for good talkers. They will not let you do a commercial but, if you can give their audience something new, informative, exciting or motivating, producers will ask you to talk about it, and may even invite you back on to their show and add you to their contacts list.

It is impossible to judge whether, or how, doing radio interviews will affect your bottom line but, provided it doesn't take too much out of your day, it is a good way to drip-feed information and subtly build a media profile.

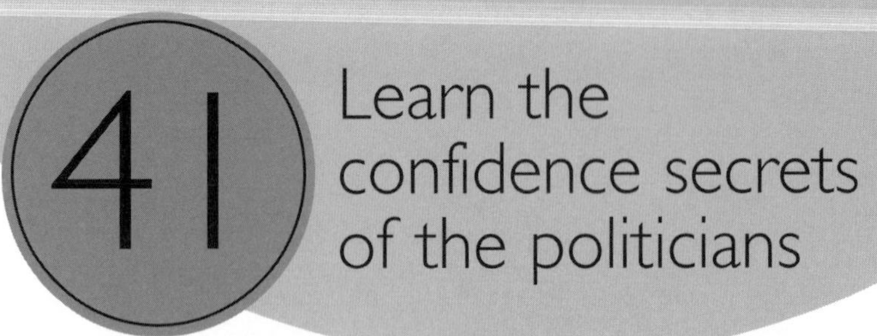

# 41 Learn the confidence secrets of the politicians

> *'I am extraordinarily patient, provided I get my own way in the end.'* Margaret Thatcher

> *'Politics have no relation to morals.'* Niccoló Machiavelli

> *'Politicians also have no leisure, because they are always aiming at something beyond political life itself, power and glory, or happiness.'* Aristotle

> *'It's going to be the year of the sharp elbow and the quick tongue.'* George W. Bush

> *'Where might is mixed with wit, there is too good an accord in a government.'* Elizabeth I

What can we learn from politicians? Some people would say, 'Not much!' Despite the bad press they receive worldwide, politicians include the most respected and venerated man of the late twentieth and early twenty-first century – Nelson Mandela. Even after 27 years of incarceration, he taught us all the importance of tolerance and forgiveness, something we should never forget. And if you think of the most influential people over the last two centuries, whether for good or bad, they are mostly politicians. Abraham Lincoln, William Wilberforce who helped abolish slavery, Winston Churchill, Mahatma Ghandi, Martin Luther King, the Kennedys and Aung San Suu Kyi all had, and have, huge influence on the world. They had the power to motivate and inspire for good. Adolf Hitler also had the ability to motivate a nation, but he used that power for evil.

It is a shame that today we tend to have little faith in the elected men and women who manage our lives. Once, everybody looked up to and revered our political leaders, but no longer. While we do need to think critically about how politicians act on our behalf, it is a pity that we no longer seem to trust those in power. This distrust breeds cynicism, and it is very difficult to motivate or inspire a population with no faith or belief to use their vote.

Politicians, when they first stand for office, usually do so with the best intentions and most MPs do a really good job. They need integrity and the courage to stick to their convictions when voting in new bills and they must stand up for their constituents, even if it means cutting the party line. MPs need to be confident communicators, as they have to be able to communicate at all levels. Voters come from all walks of life and cover ages from 18 upwards, so when they take their surgeries politicians need excellent listening skills, patience and a genuine desire to try and help their electorate. If they want to be re-elected, they need the ability to make all their constituents feel individual and unique and they also need great powers of persuasion.

## LEARN THE ART OF THE WITTY PUT-DOWN

One of the things you can learn from politicians is how to insult people – politely. Although I would not recommend insulting people for the sake of it, it is interesting to see how MPs offer a polite, or not so polite, put-down. Prime Minister Winston Churchill was famous for his wit and many other politicians have aimed some good barbs.

A former leader of the defunct SDP said of Margaret Thatcher, 'She is a heady mixture of whiskey and perfume.' Norman, now Lord, Tebbit was known for his quick wit and acid tongue. While campaigning for a fellow Conservative, he was heckled by a youth at the back of the crowd. He tried to alleviate the situation by saying 'Calm down, my lad.' The youth retorted 'You're not my Dad.' To this, Tebbit replied, 'I would quit while you're ahead, son. It's obvious I'm the only father you'll ever

1 2 3 4 5 6 7 8 9 10 11 12 13 14 15 16 17 18 19 20 21 22 23 24 25 26 27 28 29 30 31 32 33 34 35 36 37 38 39 40 41 42 43 44 45 46 47 48 49 50

know.' A comment from a Tory backbencher summed him up: 'If a wasp flew into Norman's mouth, he would sting it.' The late US President Ronald Reagan, when Governor of California, responded to a heckler who shouted 'Pig!' by replying, 'I am very proud to be called a pig. It stands for pride, integrity and guts.'

**As a politician, you have to be quick-witted, thick-skinned and tenacious.**

## PRACTISE PARLIAMENTARY COMMUNICATION SKILLS

A politican's life is demanding and requires resolve and stamina. Many debates go on into the night, so sleep is something MPs often have to do without. A new Member has to learn how to communicate in an atmosphere that sometimes resembles a bear garden; just getting heard amid the jeers and cheers can be an achievement in itself.

We trained a number of MPs when TV cameras first went into the House, which was a daunting prospect at the time. Never before had constituents so easily been able to see how their MPs performed in the Commons. For the first time they could check how many questions their elected representatives asked and how good they were when speaking, if indeed they did! We helped them with their visual image, as some of them gave their appearance little thought, evaluated their body language and developed their presentation skills. Timing is vital and MPs sometimes need the skills of a stand-up comic.

You may dismiss Prime Minister's Question Time as a spectacle, but as a piece of communication it is unrivalled. Ministers need to use all their communication tools: body language, voice projection, verbal skills and timing. They have to wait until the taunts and catcalls have died down in order to make sure their well-rehearsed points reach their audience. They have to be aware of the difference between projecting their voice and merely shouting and they need to know how to gain and keep the empathy of the audience – not an easy feat.

## EMULATE THE PASSION OF POLITICANS TO INSPIRE YOUR AUDIENCE

41

An MP is always in the spotlight, especially in the House, now that cameras are there to pick up exchanges, speeches and general body language. A weary MP caught napping does not project a very positive image, especially at election time. This is when MPs have to be at the top of their game. They need to talk to as many prospective voters as they can and this means knocking on doors, hustings and endless meetings in village halls.

It is difficult to keep up the enthusiasm for communication when you have had a hundred doors slammed in your face, but it is all part of the job. Despite the backing of a political party and the big guns brought out to help, the voters will decide who goes to Westminster on the personality and ability of the candidate. The sad thing is that ability often comes second to communication skills. A candidate who can speak well and communicate comfortably on TV and radio will get elected over another who may have more overall experience but is not so televisual.

Some MPs will dye their hair, use Botox or fix their teeth in order to make them look younger and more vigorous at election time, so they put themselves under enormous pressure. If we see an MP or minister on TV looking tired and under stress, this is not a good image, and this will be reflected in the number of votes they win. It is often the little things that can make a difference to public perception.

Both Adolf Hitler and Fidel Castro had phenomenal stamina and could stand and deliver speeches for up to eight hours at a time. It is almost impossible for us to comprehend listening to anything for that long these days, as our attention spans have definitely got shorter. Today's politicians have to bear this in mind and even the Chancellor of the Exchequer in the UK limits his budget day speech to about three hours. To inspire and motivate your audience, you need passion, and that is what good political speakers infuse into their speeches.

## Putting it all together

What we can learn from politicians is how to make our point, even against the most difficult odds. We can look at their body language and analyse the way they use words for maximum effect. We can learn from their art of timing – so important when they want to make sure they can be heard above the rabble in the House.

Politicians also have to be able to listen and they should be able to make each constituent feel special. They have to be able to delegate and deal with a host of different problems brought to them by their electorate. They have to juggle work and family life in often difficult circumstances, especially if they live a long way from Westminster. To be a competent minister, they should have exceptional powers of concentration and a wide general knowledge. They also have to be able to work long hours and look fit and healthy. Most of all, they need passion and fervour to inspire and motivate an audience.

# Get your message across in print

> *'It takes a lifetime to build a reputation and only a few seconds to destroy one.'* Warren Buffet

> *'If it's going to come out eventually, better have it come out immediately.'* Henry Kissinger

> *'The most guileful among the reporters are those who appear friendly and smile and seem to be supportive. They are the ones who will seek to gut you on every occasion.'* Edward Koch

> *'Death will be a great relief. No more interviews.'* Katharine Hepburn

> *'My husband does not like me to give interviews because I say too much. No talk, no trouble.'* Imelda Marcos

Communicating through the press means saying it like it is – in headlines that are big and bold to catch the attention. Newspapers like the *Daily Express* major in wacky headers in the vein of 'The Beast from the East!' or 'Summer Sizzler!' to describe forthcoming weather – something they know will interest readers in the UK. The other thing that attracts attention and encourages readers to pick the paper is images. Press photographers have a real talent for catching the emotions on the faces of subjects in the news, sometimes taking pictures from a long distance and in difficult circumstances.

If you are writing a presentation, looking at the way journalists use images and sum up a topic in a few well-chosen words can



9 10 11 12 13 14 15 16 17 18 19 20 21 22 23 24 25 26 27 28 29 30 31 32 33 34 35 36 37 38 39 40 41 42 43 44 45 46 47 48 49 50

give you inspiration and ideas. In other secrets, I have mentioned analysing what you see and read. Rather than just taking in the stories, look at *how* the sentences are formed and the use of adjectives in particular. Evaluate the use of pictures and how they add to the story.

It is also interesting to look at how different papers handle the same story. The tabloids are generally more sensational and attract readers who don't particularly want to go into great depth, whereas the broadsheets will usually have a more detailed analysis. Most papers are also online and will include items that might not make the paper editions, so that provides another outlet for news and information. Daily papers, whether in hard copy or online, have to be topical – old news is no news. The weekend journals and magazines, on the other hand, can publish articles that have a much longer shelf life. If you want your advert or editorial to be seen by as many people as possible, magazines can have a very long lifespan as they often end up in doctors' or dentists' waiting rooms and hang around for years.

## GET INTO PRINT AND MAKE HEADLINE NEWS!

If you want to publicize yourself, your business or an event, newspapers and magazines are still a great way to do it. Before you contact anybody, do some research: read the particular journal and see how it handles similar stories. Local papers are often a good place to start. These days the number of reporters has been cut drastically and they have very few specialists, so it is easier to get to talk to the person you need to talk to. Get to know the journalists and find out what they are looking for. Very often they will be happy for you to send in copy and pictures, so you can write your own piece.

If you want the paper to print it without too much editing, follow the style of writing as much as you can. Obviously, you cannot write an advertisement unless you want to pay for it, so you need to make sure you write with the readers in mind, as you would write for your audience for a presentation. A strong headline is vital to catch the editor's fancy, so take your time and make sure it sums up what you want to say.

## KNOW HOW TO DEAL WITH JOURNALISTS AND GET YOUR STORY STRAIGHT

The rule about talking 'off the record' is quite simple: don't do it, unless it is someone you know well and trust. Even then, only do so if you feel it is absolutely necessary. Very often, the reporter who contacted you has already written most of the story and you are being interviewed merely for a quote. However, if you inadvertently say something of interest, the interview will go deeper and more of your 'quotes' could be used, so always ask if they have talked to anyone else.

If your organization is in trouble, an article in the paper is an opportunity for damage control. There is always something to be said in mitigation. 'No comment' is regarded as a rather naive way of dealing with a reporter's questions and tends to leave an impression of evasiveness or dishonesty, so it is a good idea to say something. However, talk to your boss or colleagues first, as it is not wise to go out on a limb. Always check the journalist's credentials. They might say they are from the *Daily Mail* but actually be a freelance just pitching a story, in which case you may feel you don't want to waste your time. Listen very carefully to the questions and, in general, keep the interview short and make only statements you have prepared.

## DON'T BE CAUGHT ON THE HOP

Don't talk to a journalist who calls you out of the blue. If a reporter approaches you unexpectedly, don't say the first thing that comes into your head. Tell them you need to make some enquiries and offer to call the reporter back. In that time, determine what needs to be said and decide whether you are the right person to be saying it. If not, get someone else.

If you have attracted the attention of the press because your company is in the spotlight for some reason, try to predict what you are likely to be asked and start to prepare your response by writing bullet points that will help you remember the key factors. Newspaper reporters, especially on the national tabloids, are highly paid professionals. Their skills are not literary but investigative, and experienced reporters are skilled in the art of interrogation. Questions that can appear to be affable, or even bland, may be leading you into a trap, so beware!

Some reporters record interviews and the more experienced will ask questions without seemingly taking any notes, or they might ostentatiously put their notebook away. Be careful: the notebook may have gone but the interview will continue. Taking notes or recording the interview can inhibit interviewees, so reporters, like police officers, train themselves to make a mental note of what is said and then chat to their phone afterwards. One of the things you can do is to record the interview yourself, and tell the journalist that is what you are doing – this can intimidate them and make them more circumspect about what they print than they would otherwise be.

## Putting it all together

Generally speaking, the newspapers do not make things up, but problems can arise from their tendency to abridge, overstate or sensationalize the stories they include. The purpose of the popular press is to entertain; it is no more ominous than that, so make sure you are prepared. Always ask the journalist what the story is about. It is amazing how many times interviewees panic and get the wrong end of the stick, so make sure you understand the reporter's intentions.

The next question is to establish who else is being interviewed on the same subject. This will help you get an idea of the line of questioning. You need to ascertain the publication and when it is going to press. Where will the interview take place? Photos will literally colour the story, so make sure you are happy with the environment if a photographer is present; this is also true of TV interviews. Saying 'No comment' is not advisable, so try to say something once you have discussed things with your boss or associates.

Don't get caught on the hop. Give yourself time to think and say you will call back. Make sure you do call back, though, as journalists will say that you refused to comment, which can give the impression that you are guilty of something by default. Check the journalist's credentials, listen very carefully to the questions, keep the interview short and make only statements you have prepared.

# 43 Cope confidently with your travelling customers

> *'Do not neglect to show hospitality to strangers, for by doing that some have entertained angels without knowing it.'*
> The Bible, Hebrews 13:2

> *'It is a sin against hospitality, to open your doors and darken your countenance.'* Proverb

> *'The word "hospitality" in the New Testament comes from two Greek words. The first word means "love" and the second word means "strangers". It's a word that means love of strangers.'*
> Nancy Leigh DeMoss

> *'Delta Airlines is pleased to have some of the best flight attendants in the industry. Unfortunately, none of them are on this flight!'* Delta Airlines pilot

> *'If you work just for money, you'll never make it, but if you love what you're doing and you always put the customer first, success will be yours.'* Ray Kroc

As with the service sector, people working in the travel and hospitality industries need tolerance, fortitude, flexibility and courtesy if they are going to deliver top-class customer care. Travelling by planes, boats and trains can be stressful for passengers, who may suffer from a mixture of feelings, including nervousness, anxiety or excitement. Greeting people with a smile will reassure them as well as showing them that they are valued customers. To be able to communicate with confidence when working in the travel or hospitality sectors is a necessity when it comes to pleasing or placating people of all ages and backgrounds.

Do your research and learn as much as you can about the customers you look after because this will give you confidence and help you build a relationship with them. There is no one-size-fits-all in the travel industry: you have to deal with a broad spectrum of travellers. Children, elderly customers and disabled clientele all have specific needs and you also have to cope with cultural differences and language difficulties, which can be extremely taxing.

You have to decide what sort of a person you want to be. You can either be glum, disinterested and wrapped up in your own world or you can be smiling, outgoing and interested in everyone around you. You can choose your attitude to others and that attitude will feed back to you.

Some people can change their normal behaviour when they are part of a large group on tour. Whatever their age, they will sometimes revert to childhood and become unruly and difficult to control. You have to come across as someone who can keep calm and cope if there is a problem. An assertive, confident approach is needed in order to keep people in line. Lead by example – others will follow. As in any business, working well as a team is crucial, especially if you are in a confined place like a plane or cruise ship. Beware of gossip within the team that makes people uncomfortable or unhappy; anything that stops people enjoying their work is bad news and will affect the productivity of the organization.

## GREET YOUR PASSENGERS AND MAKE THEM FEEL WELCOME

If you are working as a member of the cabin crew, it is essential that you carry out your duties with an air of confidence, elegance, sophistication and – above all – professionalism. Flight crews have to deal with a huge variety of customers: children, different nationalities and elderly and disabled passengers. Welcoming and appreciating customers and managing difficult and delicate situations are all part of the job, as well as snack, meal and drink presentation. It is also part of your duties to look after the aircraft interior: seats, belts, soft furnishings, loos, galleys and lighting. If TV screens don't work or seats are dirty, you will get the blame, so it is up to you to keep a close eye on the condition of your aircraft and make sure it is kept up to scratch, especially the loos. On a long-haul flight, if there is no paper and they become unsavoury, it affects the perception of the flight, the airline and the cabin crew. You cannot be confident yourself if you are not confident about your environment.

It is vital to keep your uniform in good condition so that it looks clean and cared for, as it is part of your image. The better you look, the more confident you will feel and the better you will be able to communicate with your customers. Hair has to be styled for safety and neatness. (I travel so much that I notice when the crew are less than smart: if there were a Bad Hair Award, one airline would win consistently. I am thinking of donating a hairbrush for each crew!) You need to know how to handle sensitive situations with tact and diplomacy as well as knowing what to do when things go wrong.

## MAKE A POSITIVE IMPRESSION ON YOUR GUESTS

Places to stay range from guesthouses, inns, motels and hostels to pubs and hotels. While the skills needed to run these different places vary, the attitude to guests should be the same. It is a matter of getting to know your customers. The way you use your voice is crucial: a simple 'Good morning' said in a cheery tone with an accompanying smile will immediately make guests feel welcome. If you don't afford them that courtesy, plenty of other places will.

Knowing how to develop systems to run things smoothly, delivering accurate messages to guests and staff, improving your conversation and listening skills and knowing what to do if things go wrong will enable you to communicate with confidence. If you don't have these skills, make sure you acquire them. If you feel you have not had the training you need, talk to your manager and make sure you are sent on appropriate courses.

Teamwork is imperative if any establishment is to run efficiently. Key to building teams are:

- interdepartmental communication – sharing information about customer needs or complaints to prevent problems
- supporting your colleagues and treating each other with respect.

As with any form of customer service (see Secrets 36 and 37), you will appear and feel a more confident communicator if you make eye contact with guests, display good deportment and posture, read your guests' body language and put yourself in their shoes. Make sure you use the correct etiquette when speaking to customers, using their appropriate title and name. Calling a professor or doctor 'Mr' or 'Ms' can offend some people who have spent many years acquiring their moniker.

Picking up phones within the company's specified time frame (e.g. within three rings) creates an image of efficiency which generates a positive impact on prospective guests. If the phone is answered quickly, it gives the impression that service will also happen quickly, which will encourage a guest to make the booking.

## EXCEED CUSTOMER EXPECTATIONS ON GUIDED TOURS

Organizing and leading any kind of guided tour demands similar abilities to those needed elsewhere in the hospitality business and exceeding customer expectations is what you should aim for. If you are to come across as a confident tour guide, it is essential that you know what you are talking about. It may sound obvious, but you have to have a thorough knowledge of the cities and places you are visiting. Explore the location or city beforehand if possible, so that you are totally familiar with its landscape, history, local attractions, events and culture. You cannot be confident if you can't respond to obscure queries – the ones that can't be found in books or on the Internet – so you need to be fully prepared to answer all kinds of questions.

You also have to know your customers and their expectations for each particular tour and tailor the excursion to meet their individual needs. Look into potential problems so that you are prepared for them: weather, transport, catering and hotels can all pose possible difficulties, so have a backup plan just in case. Collect feedback from the customers on their opinions of the tour, as this will help you on future trips.

## Putting it all together

To succeed in the hospitality and travel industries, you need a good understanding of people and their likes and dislikes. Civility and consideration for others are essential and it is important to demonstrate the highest level of courtesy and respect towards customers and co-workers alike. Employers want staff who are confident enough in their personal interactions to establish appropriate, professional relationships with their guests and customers. You must have an excellent working knowledge of products and services as well as the cultural differences to expect on the global stage. Eye contact, good posture and a smile help provide a sincere welcome. Reading body language and putting yourself in the customers' shoes will help prevent problems.

Anticipating customers' intentions and requirements will help you exceed their expectations, which is something you should always strive to do. You need to be aware of your role in your organization and communicate this to customers as well as to peers and colleagues, as this will help you establish and maintain professional relationships. You need to feel comfortable in an environment with different cultures, languages and ethnic backgrounds.

On the service side, it is important to know how to deal with several customers at once, how to move into a group politely to attract someone's attention and how to end a conversation politely. The correct etiquette when using appropriate titles and names is vital in order not to offend anyone. Understand how to make a first and lasting impression and be an ambassador for your employer. Realize the complications of bringing personal problems to work, and try not to gossip.

1 2 3 4 5 6 7 8 9 10 11 12 13 14 15 16 17 18 19 20 21 22 23 24 25 26 27 28 29 30 31 32 33 34 35 36 37 38 39 40 41 42 43 44 45 46 47 48 49 50

# 44 Make the right impression at networking events

> *'Networking is an essential part of building wealth.'*
> Armstrong Williams

> *'It's all about people. It's about networking and being nice to people and not burning any bridges.'* Mike Davidson

> *'It isn't just what you know, and it isn't just who you know. It's actually who you know, who knows you, and what you do for a living.'* Bob Burg

> *'The way of the world is meeting people through other people.'*
> Robert Kerrigan

> *'More business decisions occur over lunch and dinner than at any other time, yet no MBA courses are given on the subject.'*
> Peter Drucker

Networking allows you to advertise yourself and your occupation, so it is an excellent way to build your business as well as enlarging your social circle. People do business with people they like and trust so, if you are a personal trainer and prospective customers can see you look professional and hear that you are competent, they are more likely to use or recommend you. This goes for any service from accounting to plumbing.

Self-confidence is essential at networking events if you are to succeed in selling yourself and your business. Going back to the 90 per cent in 20 seconds rule, it is crucial to make the right impression immediately. If you are dressed appropriately and you know you look good, you will feel confident – whether it is a social or professional occasion. Once again, a smile does more than anything else to make a positive first impression and show that you are a confident communicator. A smile is recognized in all countries and cultures and can be distinguished from at least 30 metres away.

When you first walk into the room, stand for a moment and smile. This not only makes you look like a warm, approachable and confident human being but it also gives you a chance to sum up the people there. You will automatically analyse how they are dressed, their ages and how like or unlike you they are; this will help you decide whom you should approach. You should try to look forward to any event that permits you to meet new clients, customers or friends, and see it as an opportunity. So visualize success beforehand and you will start to feel more confident.

## JOIN A GROUP WITH A CONFIDENT AIR

There is nothing worse than walking into a room where you don't know anybody and not knowing who to say hello to. Look for people who are animated and appear to be having fun rather than those immersed in chat. Don't try to enter a 'closed' group, where people are facing each other and sustaining eye contact and usually have their feet pointing towards each other. They are having a serious conversation and don't want to be interrupted.

In an 'open' group, people will be standing at a 45-degree angle to each other, providing a gap that shows they are prepared to allow another into their midst. Smile when you walk up to the group, so they know that you are looking forward to meeting them. Saying something like 'I hope I am not interrupting…' or 'Do you mind if I join you?' before giving your name helps to smooth the path. If you are at a business do, give your company name as well and say what you do. You may shake hands at this point unless people are holding food or drinks, when a nod of the head is more appropriate because you don't want them struggling with plates or glasses. Once more, it is a good plan to repeat the name of the person you are addressing – 'How do you do, Peter' or 'Hello, Lucy' – to cement the name in your mind. At networking meetings, people usually have nametags, which help you to remember names, but it is still a good idea to repeat it.

## WORK THE ROOM AND MAKE NEW CONNECTIONS

At a networking meeting, aim to work the room so that you can meet as many different people as possible. Even at a social occasion, it is good to meet new people as well as see friends, but you'll generally spend more time with friends because you are catching up rather than trying to find out whether you want to do business. However, there is no need to feel compelled to stay with anybody when you have run out of things to say.

Saying something like, 'I have really enjoyed our chat but I mustn't keep you. There must be lots of people you want to see' should give the other person the hint that you want to move on and it permits them to get away too. It is not polite to leave someone on his or her own, though, so introduce a loner to your friends before moving on.

You won't have time to do much business on the night. Arrange future meetings to discuss further business matters and be focused on what you want to achieve. If someone you are talking to gets a bit restless or begins to lose eye contact, it is a sign they are feeling trapped, so finish the conversation and move on.

## PROJECT A CONFIDENT IMAGE

Dress for success, to project the right image of your business or organization. Some clubs or hotels don't allow denim so don't wear jeans unless you are sure of the policy. Always take a tie in case you need one because not being allowed into a venue doesn't do much for your self-confidence.

Here are some tips for making the most of a networking event:

- Take plenty of business cards; it is amazing how often people forget to replenish their business card holder.
- Don't leave your phone on, as this can be distracting. If you spend time texting or having to go out of the room to answer the phone, you will be missing the chance to meet those prospective clients or possible suppliers, so make the most of the opportunity.

- Don't try to do deals there and then. You just haven't got time if you want to mix with as many people as you can. It is also unfair to monopolize others so that they can't make the most of the opportunities. Arrange to have a cup of coffee or a drink with your new associate rather than trying to do business at the time.

## Putting it all together

If you think nobody will want to talk to you, they probably won't, since a lack of confidence can make you seem uninteresting and you will subconsciously push people away. Smile as you walk into the room! Remember: we make up 90 per cent of our minds about people in about five seconds, so dress to impress; remember also that you are the image of your organization.

The correct greeting when you meet someone is still 'How do you do?' or 'Good evening'. People will judge you on a warm, firm handshake, so study yours. A handshake should be equal for both parties and both people's hands should be vertical. It ought to last no longer than five seconds and be no more than three 'pumps'. If you have wet or clammy hands, keep a tissue or handkerchief in your pocket infused with a few drops of cologne, as this can help to close the pores that make the hands damp.

To come across as a confident networker:

- don't try to enter a 'closed' group
- read the body talk and don't interrupt people mid-conversation
- engage bystanders and those on their own and introduce people to each other
- ask questions without being too personal or intrusive
- don't get stuck with one person or group for too long.

1 2 3 4 5 6 7 8 9 10 11 12 13 14 15 16 17 18 19 20 21 22 23 24 25 26 27 28 29 30 31 32 33 34 35 36 37 38 39 40 41 42 43 44 45 46 47 48 49 50

# 45 Run your family and business life smoothly

*'You can have it all. Just not all at once.'* Oprah Winfrey

*'The bad news is that you can't have it all. The good news is that when you know what's really important, you don't want it all anyway.'* Anon.

*'Can you imagine a world without men? No crime and lots of happy, fat women.'* Marion Smith

*'Sometimes I wonder if men and women really suit each other. Perhaps they should live next door and just visit now and then.'* Katharine Hepburn

*'I hate failure and that divorce was a Number One failure in my eyes. It was the worst period of my life. Neither Desi nor I have been the same since, physically or mentally.'* Lucille Ball

Companies expect 100 per cent from their employees, and as our salaries increase so do our responsibilities, just at the time in our lives when we frequently also have family commitments. It seems unfair that some women feel they have to say they are leaving early to go to the dentist rather than admit to having a sick child at home. Certainly, for men or women, trying to do the washing, shopping and cooking as well as creating a positive image at work is not the easiest of tasks. Supporting our children in their various activities, both during and after school, also takes a lot of juggling. If you have the sort of job that leaves you over-tired, stressed and unable to take your mind off problems at the office, you will not succeed either domestically or professionally.

It is essential for working parents to have the best possible childcare arrangements in place when they return to work, as it is impossible to function happily and efficiently if you are worried about what may be happening at home. Both men and women find being awake most of the night looking after small children challenging and it is tempting to rush into the office, clothes creased and hair unwashed, but this is not the confident image you need to project. Prioritizing your time is vital if your family and business life is to run smoothly.

## SHARE AND VALUE FAMILY LIFE WITH YOUR PARTNER

Some couples have reversed the traditional roles, with the father staying at home to look after children while the mother goes out to work. Certainly, most young women today expect their partner to share household jobs and take an active role in bringing up children. If a man or a woman is made to feel that looking after home and children is not a priority, the children are the ones who will suffer.

To come home every night when the children are asleep is a terrible sacrifice but it has become the norm for more and more working parents. In these days of equality, couples need to decide who is going to progress faster up the career path and therefore earn more, and that partner will be the breadwinner. Whoever it is, couples have to make allowances for each other and ensure that they both have time to enjoy the children as well as benefiting materially. For a man (or a woman) to be given 'housekeeping' money in a way that depletes their self-image devalues the vital role that one partner has to play in order for the household to function healthily.

Running a house is excellent training for the workplace and gives experience that can be of enormous benefit to men and women returning to work. Managing household chores and arrangements makes you an expert in time management and gives you valuable organizational skills. If you're running the household, it is important to maintain outside interests, as well as continuing to be included in any decision-making. It is essential that both partners feel equally

significant and share responsibilities. To retain good relationships, partners need to show how much they value each other and give each other the support they need. Effective communication is essential to find the arrangement that is right for your family.

## PROJECT A POSITIVE IMAGE ABOUT YOUR CAREGIVING ROLE

It's very easy to feel that you aren't contributing if you don't have a career. However, as most people realize, bringing up a family is one of the most important jobs there is, and that's how you should look at it. The positive image you project will mean that you are taken seriously. If you are lucky enough to be able to look after your children yourself and you don't want to work outside the home, why not make the most of it?

It is imperative, though, not to lose touch with what is going on in the world. As discussed in previous secrets, it is important to create a wide social circle that will also include your partner. Take up hobbies, learn a language, restart activities that are not just related to the children and that will get you out of the house, improve your general knowledge and make yourself use your brain.

Many women who have devoted themselves to bringing up a family and supported their partner reach the age of 40 and look into the mirror and think, 'What have I done with my life?' They have made a valuable contribution to society, but what have they done for themselves? Many marriages break up if the only thing that has kept the couple together has been the children, and once they have flown the nest there is nothing left.

## HANDLE A DIVORCE AS BEST YOU CAN

When a relationship breaks down, sometimes separation or divorce is the only option, but it is vital to make sure the door is always left open if at all possible. Try not to say things you might regret in the heat of the moment and, if you do, apologize! This may sound tricky but, even if you say you are sorry by text or email, it might help the relationship end in a civilized manner – and you never know when you might come up against your ex again, or in what circumstances.

If children are involved, it is vital that partners don't denigrate each other. Children will often blame themselves for break-ups, which is heartbreaking, so don't criticize their other parent. Be as civil as you can; remember that their blood runs in your children's veins too. It is possible to develop a different relationship with your ex and eventually be able to spend family days together with children and grandchildren. Bear in mind the wider family, too. A break-up is even more distressing for children if they can no longer see grandparents, aunts, uncles and cousins. Even if you can't bear your ex and their kin, you do not have the right to deprive your children of their wider family.

If there are no children involved, it is easier in some ways, but every break-up is painful and can sap your confidence. Some relationships break up after a long time and it is difficult for people to pick up the threads of their lives. In this case, take up a new hobby, learn a new skill and join a dating agency if you want to meet completely new people.

### Putting it all together

Being able to relate to different people on different levels is all part of becoming a confident communicator. Relating to your partner is vital for a happy and harmonious life at home. If both partners work, there should be give and take as far as sharing household tasks and looking after the children are concerned. If one or other partner stays at home to look after the children, they should be given equal respect and consideration and not made to feel like a second-class citizen. To retain good relationships, partners need to show how much they value each other and give each other the support they need.

Divorce is a misfortune for any family but try to maintain a civilized relationship with your ex if you possibly can. Never criticize your partner in front of your children; remember that they share the same DNA.

1 2 3 4 5 6 7 8 9 10 11 12 13 14 15 16 17 18 19 20 21 22 23 24 25 26 27 28 29 30 31 32 33 34 35 36 37 38 39 40 41 42 43 44 45 46 47 48 49 50

# 46 Know how to talk to children to boost their confidence

*'Most bad behaviour comes from insecurity.'* Debra Winger

*'We cannot fashion our children after our desires, we must have them and love them as God has given them to us'.* Johann Wolfgang Von Goethe

*'Most of us become parents long before we have stopped being children.'* Mignon McLaughlin

*'Parents are the last people on earth who ought to have children.'* Samuel Butler

*'Children should be led into the right paths, not by severity, but by persuasion.'* Terence

Conversations with children are fascinating: they have the most original thoughts and ideas, especially before they start their formal education. I talk to quite a number of children – my own relatives and the ones I teach. While talking is important, it is vital to listen to children – and listen carefully. It is so easy, when taking them to and from school, for example, to say simply 'yes' and 'no' and have your mind on other things, but you can use this time as an opportunity for real communication.

A child needs special time with its parents when a new baby comes along. We all hope our first-born will be delighted to have a sibling to play with, but many young children don't take kindly to the arrival of someone who seems to take their parents' focus away from their universe. We can talk to them all we like before the event, show them the pram and give them their own dolly as their 'baby' but, if you don't give them the most precious thing you have, your time and attention, after the baby arrives, you could be in for a rocky ride.

A good time to talk to children is after their bedtime story. It can be difficult when you are tired and still haven't made dinner, but spending that extra time with each child individually pays dividends. Chatting with them at bedtime gives them the chance to ask questions and discuss problems that they might not want to share with anyone else.

Trust is vital if you are going to communicate well with children. Always keep your promises – if you say you are going to do something, do it and let them know you have done it. After the age of about eight or nine years old, children become much more self-conscious and more easily embarrassed, often becoming less extrovert, so careful communication at this time will pay dividends when they get to their teenage years.

## DON'T PLAY THE BLAME GAME

Children blame themselves for many things, sometimes things that parents or guardians are unaware of. This is especially true when it comes to relationships breaking down or the loss of a loved one. Most people who have been through a divorce are acutely aware that their children might have felt that they were somehow to blame, and tried to make sure that they understood that it had absolutely nothing to do with them. Nonetheless, this often fails to help children realize that they are not responsible in some way for a break-up. It is important to give them enough information but not too much. It is unfair to share every detail – young children can't understand and older children often don't want to know because it makes them feel uncomfortable.

Never denigrate or belittle your partner – he or she is your child's flesh and blood and it can do lasting damage to children's self-esteem in later life. Saying 'You are just like your father/mother' to a child can be both hurtful and confusing if you have just derided that person and called them all the names under the sun. Older children will also blame themselves if something happens to younger siblings, so they need to be reassured that they were not responsible, if that is the case.

## PRAISE THEM, PRAISE THEM, PRAISE THEM!

The greatest thing you can give your children is confidence in themselves and confidence in the fact that you love them unconditionally. There is so much emphasis on physical perfection and achieving goals that many children, even those as young as seven or eight, can begin to feel inadequate. You must be honest, however: telling them that they are the most beautiful person in the world and cleverer than everyone else is no good because they know it isn't true and will begin to lose faith in you.

Pick out the things they are good at. Everyone has a talent and that needs to be explored and encouraged. Praise them as much as you can. It is so easy to get caught up in the 'Don't do that' cycle and, while discipline is essential to make children feel secure as well as to teach them that the world does not revolve just around them, they should be praised when they do the small things as well as the bigger ones. Thank them and say 'please', as you would to an adult; you are their role model and you need to lead by example.

## SHOW CHILDREN THAT RULES ARE RULES

As parents, you must show solidarity with each other in front of your children and be clear that no means no. It's therefore important to decide on rules and boundaries and stick to them. If one parent says no and the other gives in, it is not only confusing for the child, but that child quickly learns how to manipulate the system. Try not to argue about anything to do with these rules of behaviour in front of the children. Even if you are tempted to make your point, it is better to say nothing at the time but talk to your partner calmly later, when the children are in bed.

It is also vital to lead by example, which means speaking to your partner kindly and with respect. If the children hear you shouting at each other downstairs, what sort of message is it sending them? You are the prime role models for your children and they will tend to copy your behaviour.

Children should be taught to read body language from an early age. If they learn that, when grown-ups are in conversation, they will be listened to if they wait for a gap in the chat, they will quickly realize that that is the best way to get attention. If, however, an adult is preoccupied with the paper or watching TV and seems uninterested in them, it is not surprising that a child will make a fuss until somebody does listen.

Teachers also make an enormous impression, both positive and negative, on children and having to cope with challenging pupils every day is a real skill. Parents should try to back the teachers up if at all possible when there are disciplinary issues, as children quickly learn how to divide and rule. As a teacher, the way you dress is important: students are summing you up as much as you are assessing them so, if you look confident, well groomed, stylish and up to the minute, you are much more likely to gain their respect than if you look as though you don't care. Negotiation rather than discipline is the norm in many schools and, to gain control of the class, you have to portray a really confident image in order to keep students' attention. Yet again, a smile makes all the difference if you want to get children on your side, especially the young ones.

## Putting it all together

If you look after children as a parent, carer or teacher, it is vital to convey confidence. This helps children feel secure and give them the belief that the world is a safe place and that you, the adult, can be trusted to be consistent. Being aware of their individuality and teaching them how to communicate with others will give children the self-confidence they need to go out in the world and achieve their dreams.

Always answer children when they ask questions or want to speak to you. This doesn't mean letting them interrupt every few minutes but, if they keep on saying 'Mummy, mummy, mummy' and you ignore them, they will always interrupt because that is the only way they will eventually get your attention. If you are in conversation, ask them to wait until you have finished talking and tell them you will answer their question then.

There are several ways you can teach children to be polite when trying to attract attention. Saying 'Excuse me' can backfire because they might think it gives them carte blanche to interrupt whenever they like, so teaching them how to read body language so that they can tell when adults don't want to be interrupted is a very good lesson for life – as well as for saving your sanity! Show them the different stances people adopt when they are deep in discussion. Teach them to realize that, if someone doesn't answer after a minute or so, it is because they are engrossed in conversation and don't want to be disturbed. This will also improve their social skills and help them with their own friendships and relationships.

# 47 Talk to teens so they will talk to you

> *'The young always have the same problem – how to rebel and conform at the same time. They have now solved this by defying their parents and copying one another.'* Quentin Crisp

> *'The best way to keep children at home is to make the home atmosphere pleasant, and let the air out of the tyres.'* Dorothy Parker

> *'As a teenager you are at the last stage in your life when you will be happy to hear that the phone is for you.'* Fran Lebowitz

> *'The invention of the teenager was a mistake. Once you identify a period of life in which people get to stay out late but don't have to pay taxes – naturally, no one wants to live any other way.'* Judith Martin

> *'The average teenager still has all the faults his parents outgrew.'* Anon.

Teenagers are probably some of the most difficult people to communicate with. When children reach their teens, they tend to think they know all there is to know about life, and anyone over the age of 25 has had it. But, if you build a good listening relationship with your children when they are young, you should find the bumpy road through the teenage years a little smoother. However, hormones and peer pressure can turn your little angel into a veritable demon. The main thing is not to take it too personally. Very often, parents are the only people they can vent their frustrations on, and any communication is better than none!



9 10 11 12 13 14 15 16 17 18 19 20 21 22 23 24 25 26 27 28 29 30 31 32 33 34 35 36 37 38 39 40 41 42 43 44 45 46 47 48 49 50

So how can you communicate confidently with a sullen teenager? While you should never try to be a 'big brother or sister', it is useful to keep abreast of their favourite TV programmes, music, computer games and other interests, so that you can chat to them on their level. They won't want to hear stories about life when you were a teenager (unless the stories are sensational!), and you don't want them to think you live in the past.

Involving your child in setting boundaries is a good way to help them understand why you have the expectations that you do. Look at the boundaries other families set and discuss what is good and not so good, what is reasonable and what is not. Discuss what's appropriate for your family, and why. Some families have regular meetings to discuss the perimeters to see if they are still fair or whether things need to change. You can then adjust them if needed. If your children make a case for changing your family's boundaries, pay attention; even if you disagree, listen carefully to their reasons and what they have to say.

## FEED TEENAGERS AND THEN CHOOSE YOUR BATTLES

One thing I have learned about teenagers is that you don't talk to them about anything important until after food. This is especially true of boys. There is a German adage that says a young man has a wolf in his belly, so feed him first! It is also worth bearing in mind that males and females communicate in different ways. Women (and teenage girls) will use up to 15,000 words and gestures a day whereas men (and teenage boys) will only use about 5,000. So, if your son has been out, he has probably used most of his words for the day, and the minute he walks through the door is not the time to confront him.

There is no doubt that teenagers can be infuriating, but it is important to try not to get angry about everything. Be selective about what you take issue with. Don't get annoyed about trivial things; remember, it could be worse! Remind yourself that they are still very young and it's OK for them not to have a clue what they want to do when they are still at school. If you can help them form their life plan, so much the better, but understand that they do have plenty of time.

## BUILD TRUST AND SHOW YOUR LOVE

It is vital to build or rebuild trust with your youngsters. Learn when to wait for them to come to you, and learn when to jump in to help. You need to keep an eye on them without them realizing that they are being watched. You also need to know when to offer reminders of your complete love for them, no matter what they do. Listen empathetically. Use open questions. Rather than saying 'Why did you do that?', try 'Tell me in your own words why you did that, so that I can understand.' Don't condemn or be judgemental without listening to their side of the story first. Put yourself in their shoes; none of us likes being told what to do all the time.

Embarrassment, guilt and fear can stop your teenagers talking to you. Bullying, for example, is still rife in schools, despite the measures taken to stamp it out, but most children will not talk about it at home. However, you can watch for the signs: if your child becomes withdrawn or starts to play truant, find out why. Talk to teachers or talk to their friends. This must be done with tact and diplomacy, because they don't want to be seen breaking confidences. Peer pressure to drink, take drugs or have sex can be overwhelmingly strong, so take it seriously. Talk to your teen and try to read their body talk and see how often they make eye contact. Get him or her to open up by asking questions: 'If a friend was in a difficult situation, how would you help?' and see what reaction you get.

## DEVELOP SOME COMMON GROUND

Try to develop some common ground. Listening to their music is a good start, or you could ask them about their heroes and role models. Ask them why they like them and what they admire about them. This can give you an insight into their views and how they think. Compare your philosophy and culture to theirs, both the good and bad points. By all means tell them about your experiences if it will help them see you as someone who thinks in a similar way to them, and not someone living in a different era. You need to narrow the gap between you and your teenagers.

If you catch your child smoking or drinking, don't over-react. It depends on your family boundaries as to whether you let

1 2 3 4 5 6 7 8 9 10 11 12 13 14 15 16 17 18 19 20 21 22 23 24 25 26 27 28 29 30 31 32 33 34 35 36 37 38 39 40 41 42 43 44 45 46 47 48 49 50

your older teenagers drink alcohol; if you do, suggest they have a drink with dinner. Try to discourage smoking, but there is little point in punishing them by cutting off their allowance because that is almost bound to make them smoke even more. If you feel you cannot get through to them, try emailing your objections and concerns about their behaviour.

**Furthermore**

A good place to talk to teens is when you are driving them somewhere in the car. They are stuck with you for some time but, as you are looking at the road, you are not scrutinizing them and this gives them freedom to open up to you.

## Putting it all together

What may seem trivial to you as a parent may be something big to your teenager, so take their concerns seriously. Help them analyse their friendships and give them tips rather than advice, so that they don't feel they are being lectured to. Build trust so that they know they can talk to you at any time about anything. Never tell them off in the heat of the moment if you can help it. Think carefully about what you say to them so that it can't be misconstrued, as teenagers will often try to find a way to turn what you say into criticism.

You cannot change what you don't acknowledge, so analyse your children's behaviour and face the facts if they are drinking, smoking or taking drugs. Teenagers worry about what their friends think and peer pressure can often be overwhelming. Take action and get professional help if necessary. Remember, there is power in forgiveness. We teach people how to treat us, so treat your children with respect and they are more likely to return the compliment.

A cry from many teenagers is that parents don't listen but just criticize, so make sure you give your children the time and respect to state their views and opinions. They are young adults and need to be treated and listened to as such.

# 48 Keep fit to gain confidence

*'I've got mad energy for days. That's what people can't get their minds around. They say, "Oh, he's going to crash." They try to apply all these common terms to a guy who is not common. I don't fit into their little box.'* Charlie Sheen

*'Medicines are only fit for old people.'* Napoleon Bonaparte

*'The trouble with always trying to preserve the health of the body is that it is so difficult to do without destroying the health of the mind.'* G. K. Chesterton

*'The greatest wealth is health.'* Virgil

*'Poor health is not caused by something you don't have; it's caused by disturbing something that you already have. Healthy is not something that you need to get, it's something you have already if you don't disturb it.'* Dean Ornish

We are familiar with the adage that a fit body generates a fit mind and eventually we learn that it is absolutely true. If you feel sluggish and are lacking in 'get-up-and-go', it affects everything you do. You won't rise to new challenges or take on extra commitments if you don't have the energy. Feeling unfit also depletes confidence because, if you don't feel good about yourself, your self-esteem will suffer. To create a positive image, we must portray fitness and vitality.

First of all, you have to examine why you are unfit. It is usually lack of exercise and a poor diet (see Secret 49 for advice on



9 10 11 12 13 14 15 16 17 18 19 20 21 22 23 24 25 26 27 28 29 30 31 32 33 34 35 36 37 38 39 40 41 42 43 44 45 46 47 48 49 50

nutrition). Many of us live a sedentary lifestyle these days: if we work in an office, we are likely to spend hours at a desk every day, and many of us spend our evenings sitting on the sofa to watch TV or browse the Internet. We may also tend to drive everywhere or go by public transport rather than walk.

There are some very simple remedies to help you get fit that don't necessarily involve going to the gym or running for miles. If you don't play much sport, try using a bike instead of the car and take the stairs rather than the lift. Run up escalators, or take the stairs instead. Something as simple as stretching regularly can help relieve muscle strain and enable you to take a good lungful of air and this will give you a quick burst of energy.

As we get older we tend to shrink a little, so stretching as high as you can every morning and evening will help keep your back and shoulders in good order. This is particularly important if you work on a computer every day.

**Furthermore**

To remedy my deskbound existence, I have bought myself a mini trampoline and put it in the office next to my desk so that I can have a quick bounce every hour or so. You can work out your own routines or download some from the Internet. For me, it works really well.

## GO FOR IT!

If you are unfit or have damaged muscles or joints, walking and swimming are the best forms of exercise because you can start slowly and build up your fitness gradually. Make sure you have properly cushioned shoes if you are going to do a lot of walking or decide to try jogging. Riding horses is good exercise and provides fresh air and exhilaration, but a word of warning: if you haven't ridden for some time, go easy to begin with, as you use muscles you don't seem to use for anything else! Fencing is an extremely good way of keeping fit and it is good fun too. Yoga, Pilates and ballet help promote grace and elegance as well as keeping you supple and getting you fit. If you like dancing, then dance your way to fitness with a dance fitness class such as Zumba. If a class would make you feel uncomfortable, you can dance in the privacy of your home – simply put on your favourite music and dance!

**As in other areas of life, trying a new activity to increase your fitness is an invaluable way of increasing your confidence and hence your communication skills.**

## PLAY A GAME FOR A GOOD WORKOUT

Being good at any game will build your confidence and, if you become a captain of a team, you are forced to become a confident communicator in order to plan, motivate, cajole and inspire. Games like rugby, football, hockey, lacrosse and squash are a very good way of keeping fit.

Tennis provides a good workout in short, sharp bursts and it is also a very social game that you can carry on playing well into your dotage. Playing golf will also help you keep fit and is a great way to widen your social circle at the same time. This is another game that you can play for as long as you can walk and hold a club. You can also play it by yourself, which is not the case for most ball games.

## EXERCISE AT HOME TO MUSIC

If you can't bear the thought of jogging and you can't get to a gym, there are exercises you can do at home. If you haven't got a fitness plan and you don't have much time, put on your favourite music (it helps keep the rhythm) and try this simple routine. Even ten minutes three times a week can really help improve your fitness.

1. Always start by gently warming up. This can be either marching on the spot or stepping on and off the bottom stair or a shallow step for about four minutes. Next comes the stretch. Try to touch the ceiling! Reach up as high as you can until you feel your spine lengthen, being careful not to push your head back too far, as this can strain the neck. Do this to the count of 20.

2. Stand with your legs apart, put your hands on your hips and keeping your back straight, bend your knees no more than 90 degrees, keeping them in line with the toes. Try this 20 times.
3. Keep your hands on your hips, back straight, and gently swing the body from side to side, again 20 times.
4. Put your hands in the air and stretch up, then drop your arms towards your toes; lower your head and shoulders towards the floor with knees slightly bent. Try this ten times.
5. Place your fingertips together, level with your chest, and push out 20 times. Next, spread your arms out and back another 20 times.
6. Stretch your arms in front, cross them at the wrist with palms facing, and then clasp your hands together. Raise both arms above your head and lift them as high as you can. Now stretch them 20 times.
7. Lie flat on the floor and bring each knee up to your chin in turn, 20 times.
8. Stay on the floor with your knees bent. Flatten the hollow of your back into the floor, pulling your tummy tight. Gently lift your head and shoulders a little, 20 times.
9. Stand up slowly, hold on to a sturdy piece of furniture (a table or a chest of drawers) with both hands, arms outstretched, and raise one leg behind you, then the other. Repeat 20 times.
10. Run on the spot for as long as you can before it feels uncomfortable.

These are short and sweet, but they exercise every part of your body and will increase your fitness over time.

## Putting it all together

Keeping fit is vital for confidence but it is essential to choose a way of getting fit that you will enjoy because, if you don't like it, you won't do it. There are many sports to choose from to get you fit that are challenging, competitive or purely enjoyable. Choose one that suits you. For workout routines at home, choose music that has a steady beat – not too fast or too slow – as it is essential that you are comfortable with the speed of each exercise.

If you would prefer to work out at home rather than join a gym or a club, there are all kinds of fitness tapes and DVDs available, so try to find one that works for you. If you are at all worried about health factors, see your doctor before starting any fitness regime.

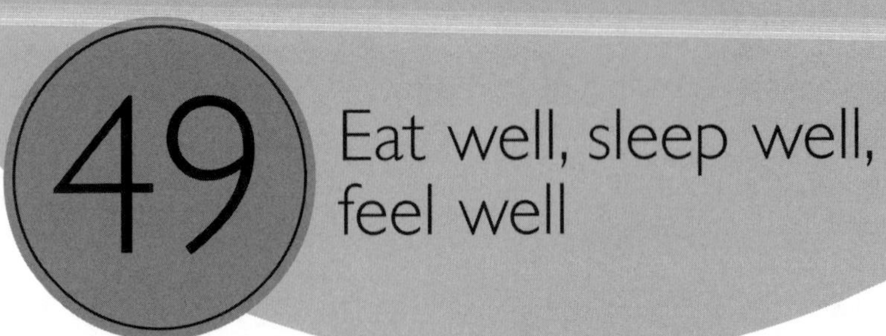

# 49 Eat well, sleep well, feel well

> *'The way you think, the way you behave, the way you eat, can influence your life by 30 to 50 years.'* Deepak Chopra

> *'To avoid sickness eat less; to prolong life worry less.'* Chu Hui Weng

> *'If you can't sleep, then get up and do something instead of lying there worrying. It's the worry that gets you, not the lack of sleep.'* Dale Carnegie

> *'There is more refreshment and stimulation in a nap, even of the briefest, than in all the alcohol ever distilled.'* Edward Lucas

> *'If you're happy, if you're feeling good, then nothing else matters.'* Robin Wright

A good regime is not just about eating and sleeping, it is about self-esteem and feeling great. It may be a bit of a lifestyle change, but getting into the habit of eating well and getting enough sleep will give you more energy, help you feel better about yourself and keep you in tip-top condition. There is a lot of truth in the saying: 'If you look after your stomach for the first 50 years, it will look after you for the next 50.' When you are young, you can eat what you like, when you like, without feeling ill effects, but don't underestimate the damage you can do to your digestive system in the long run, which could affect you in later life. There are now more concoctions produced for intestinal disorders than for heart conditions, apparently.

Sleep is also vitally important for wellbeing. Lack of proper sleep can lead to obesity and heart disease because the body compensates for a lack of energy by sending signals that you are hungry, so people tend to go for a quick fix, gorging on unhealthy foods such as chocolate or crisps. Sleep allows the brain to compute the matters of the day and that 'downtime' is also when the cells in our body renew themselves.

As your brain is governed by your 'inner voice', how you speak to yourself can have a dramatic effect on the way you manage your diet and sleep patterns. If you worry before you go to bed about not being able to sleep, you are planting those negative thoughts into your brain and you probably won't sleep. It is the same with your diet. If you concentrate on the things you shouldn't eat, those are the things you will crave, so tell yourself that you are dying to eat more fruit and veg, and that will work too.

## CHOOSE A DIET FOR VITAL LIVING

To radiate confidence, you have to be convinced that you are looking good and feeling good from the inside out. What we put into our bodies has an important effect on our sense of wellbeing.

One of the crucial things is to *appreciate* your food. Looking at food and eating slowly as well as chewing properly enables you to digest it properly. As the digestive process starts with your saliva, you need your mouth to water, hence the saying 'we eat with our eyes'. Eating slowly also allows you to be aware of when you have had enough. So tell yourself how much you are going to benefit from what is in front of you and sit down and enjoy it!

Essentially, the food we eat is divided into three main types:

- **Proteins** – meat, milk, cheese, butter, eggs, fish, nuts, coconut, olives.
- **Carbohydrates** – potatoes, rice, bread, cereals, grains, squashes, pulses, beans.
- **Fruit and vegetables** – these can also be split into several types, but for simplicity they can be put into one category.

As we are made up of 80 per cent water, it seems logical that we should eat plenty of foods containing a high proportion of water. Fruit is about 90 per cent water, so it helps to cleanse the body, and it also contains fructose, which is quickly converted into glucose, the energy we need for our brains. Fresh or freshly squeezed fruit juice (especially orange or apple) is therefore good for getting the brain going quickly as well as for starting off the process of cleansing the body and renewing the cells. So, for anti-ageing from the inside out, start your day with fruit. However, once fruit or vegetables are juiced they convert into sugar rather than fructose, which can harm teeth, so, if you always juice them rather than eating them whole, you are losing out on fibre and nutrients from the skins.

Drinking water helps clear the system of toxins and helps fill a hunger gap between meals. Drinking a couple of glasses of water before a meal can prevent overeating by curbing the appetite. You do not need to drink huge amounts of water, but a litre a day is probably the minimum everyone should drink, and still water is better than sparkling. If just drinking plain water doesn't seem particularly enticing, try adding a few slices of lemon, orange, mint or ginger to a jug of water and leaving it in the fridge overnight. Hot water with a slice of lemon or ginger is also good for clearing toxins.

**Furthermore**

If you like a drink, moderation is essential. Wine – especially red wine – is better for you than spirits, and it's a good idea to have at least two alcohol-free days a week.

## SLEEP TIGHT

As mentioned, getting enough sleep is vital to feeling good and feeling good is vital to feeling confident. We cannot function if we are really tired, but sleep doesn't always come easily even when we feel sleepy. However, there are several things we can do to make it more likely that we get enough rest and the type of deep sleep we need to restore the body.

If you have trouble either getting to sleep or staying asleep, here are a few tips:

- Finish eating at least three hours before you go to bed.
- If you find your mind racing as soon as your head hits the pillow, stop watching TV about an hour beforehand.
- Avoid having a 'nightcap' at bedtime, thinking that this will help you get a good night's sleep. Although alcohol is a short-term sedative, it is also a stimulant, so you are likely to wake up after about three or four hours and find sleep even more elusive.
- Don't drink caffeinated coffee or tea after about 4 p.m.
- Ensure your bed is warm and comfortable and turn the mattress regularly. We spend on average a third of our lives in bed, so make sure yours is in good condition and change it as soon as it gets a bit spongy.
- Keep your bedroom cool and dark, especially in the summer.

If you have trouble getting to sleep, don't go to bed until you feel really tired, and don't get into the habit of falling asleep in front of the TV or while reading a book.

## FEEL GREAT!

If your overall health is good, and you take enough exercise, eat the right food and get enough sleep, you will feel great! You will be proud of your body as your skin and hair will glow with health and vitality. And, if you feel good, you will feel confident.

## Putting it all together

It seems that there is no need to drink gallons of water, but it is important to keep the body hydrated, especially if you have a lot of salt in your diet. If you want to lose weight, try drinking two glasses of water before each meal. This will quench your thirst and also help suppress hunger. If you fancy an alcoholic drink, sit down and relax, as this is also essential for wellbeing. However, the more alcohol you drink, the less weight you will lose because it not only contains calories but also inhibits the burning of excess fat.

To lose weight, it is also important not to eat carbohydrate after 6 p.m. and to eat nothing at all after 9 p.m. at the latest – otherwise it gives the body no time to digest the food before sleep. If you feel the need to eat between meals, fruit or carrots and celery sticks are good and, for a treat, a piece of 80 per cent organic chocolate.

If you have trouble getting to sleep, try getting up half an hour earlier than normal and take more exercise. The main thing is not to stress about it. Nothing is more likely to keep you awake than worrying that you can't sleep. If this happens, use relaxation techniques to help: lie very still and contemplate each part of your body, starting with your toes. Relax each joint and muscle, moving slowly up your body – ankles, calves, knees, thighs, pelvis, abdomen and chest. Then relax your fingers, wrists, elbows and shoulders before moving on to your chin, mouth, facial muscles, eyes, forehead and scalp. If you really concentrate, this exercise genuinely works and will release the tension from your body, allowing you to sink into sleep.

# 50 Enjoy being a confident communicator

> *'It took me a long time not to judge myself through someone else's eyes.'* Sally Field

> *'They can because they think they can.'* Virgil

> *'Great are they who see that spiritual is stronger than any material force, that thoughts rule the world.'* R.W. Emerson

> *'I am not a has-been. I am a will be.'* Lauren Bacall

> *'Confidence comes not from always being right but from not fearing to be wrong.'* Peter T. Mcintyre

This book has given you the hints and tips you need to become a confident communicator, wherever you are and whomever you are with. To build true confidence, you have to love and appreciate yourself, so every morning look into the mirror and say the following: 'You don't look too bad at all – in fact, you look very good. Remember – there is no one else in the world like you, you are unique and today *is* going to be a really good day!'

Self-esteem and appreciation of yourself mean being happy in your own skin. Whatever our size and shape, we need to recognize that we all have something special to offer the world. We are generally extremely critical of ourselves – very few of us like our own bodies. Our hair is too thin, our eyes are too small or our waistline is too big. Some things we can change and some things we can't (not without expensive surgery, anyway), so the



9 10 11 12 13 14 15 16 17 18 19 20 21 22 23 24 25 26 27 28 29 30 31 32 33 34 35 36 37 38 39 40 41 42 43 44 45 46 47 48 49 50

road to happiness and contentment is to make the most of what we have and minimize what we don't like. The more you can do this, the better the days will get.

**Furthermore**

What you think will determine who you are and what you become. This is not to say that, if you follow this mantra, life will be perfect and nothing will go wrong, but it will help you gain a more positive attitude towards yourself and your qualities.

Always bear in mind that, if you don't appreciate yourself, nobody else will. Concentrate on your good points and make the most of them and be comforted by the reality that there is probably no one in the world who is completely happy with how they look. What is important is what is on the inside. If you think negative thoughts, it will show on your face. Since far more muscles are needed to produce a frown than a smile, you might as well smile. When you smile, positive signals are sent to the brain, which makes it difficult to feel depressed, so try smiling more, especially when you meet people. Smiling does wonders when forging relationships.

## ACCENTUATE THE POSITIVE

Positive thinking is vital; remember the adage: 'If you think you can – you can!' Also, take time for yourself. A long bath, a relaxing facial, a workout in the gym or a walk with the dog can help ease tension and allow you time to think about yourself and what you want from life. Spend time on deciding what clothes suit your colouring and your body shape. Experiment with hairstyles and make-up and build your own brand. Developing your unique style will give you confidence and walking tall, standing straight and looking people in the eye will portray that confidence to others – as will a smile.

Being courteous and having good manners are important if you are to communicate well with others. Knowing how to be tactful and understanding the difference between being assertive and aggressive are vital to effective communication.

Look for good, positive role models and learn from them. Anyone in the public eye has something to teach us all, whether it is positive or negative.

## ELIMINATE THE NEGATIVE

Get rid of negative childhood influences and also be careful of friendships that pull you down. Aim to surround yourself with 'radiators' rather than 'drains'. Try not to let life's brickbats leave you depressed. Having lost two people I loved very much within six weeks of each other, I have learned always to look forward. My life changed for ever, but positive things have come from the heartbreak. Don't stop thinking about tomorrow and look for all the things that are still good in your life. You cannot change the past, so don't keep going back over it unless there is a lesson you can learn. Worrying about what you cannot change will only make you miserable and deplete your self-confidence, so look for the positive people and events all around you – they are there.

Your 'inner voice' or unconscious mind governs everything you think and all the actions you take. If you expect negative things to happen, they will. For example, when I began riding horses again after a break of about 20 years, I had recurrent fears that I would fall off. All my past experiences of falling off came flooding back and, sure enough, I did fall off, dislocating my shoulder. But the stupid thing was that I saw myself doing it, so I almost made it happen.

**Discard the negative thoughts in your mind and begin to think only constructive thoughts.**

## GO ON – ENJOY LIFE!

Life is for living and you may as well enjoy it! It is a wise idea to try to live for and love each day as it comes, because you never know what is around the corner. This doesn't mean that you don't plan for the future: of course you should create your life strategy, but enjoying every day as much as you can develops a positive attitude and a happy disposition, which is an invaluable approach to life.

**Preparation is the key to confidence and confidence is the key to success, so prepare!**

Here are some key strategies for increasing your enjoyment of life:

- Whether you are making a speech, hosting a party or chairing a board meeting for the first time, thorough preparation will give you the confidence to deliver the goods and even enjoy the event.
- Expand your mind by reading and learning new skills. We should carry on learning all our lives; once you stop learning you might as well be dead.
- Keeping fit is central to enjoying true confidence. If you look at the stairs and have to take a deep breath before you tackle them, you need to start taking more exercise. The fitter you are, the more energy you have and the more you will enjoy life.
- Eating well is also crucial to good health. Making sure you have your 'five a day' at least and try to eat food that is as fresh as possible.

If you feel your diet is lacking and you need to take vitamins or mineral supplements, see what works for you. There are conflicting views about supplements but I always take them in the winter or when I spend a lot of time on a plane. I have sat next to people coughing and spluttering for eight hours or more and haven't caught a bug yet, so they obviously work for me – and, if I tell myself they will work, they will!

## Putting it all together

Time is one of the most precious things you can give anyone, especially your partner and your children. Take time to listen and give them the time to hear themselves think, so that you can talk about their hopes, fears or concerns. This is equally true with colleagues and staff at work. So many problems can be avoided if people are encouraged to voice their worries or ideas in a non-critical and empathetic environment. Good managers listen more than they talk. Prepare thoroughly and visualize success. Look outside your box and try new sports or hobbies and find new interests. All these things help you meet people, make new friends and become a confident communicator. Above all, 'always look on the bright side of life', as the song says and you will find things do get brighter.

They say the human nervous system or brain cannot tell the difference between a powerfully imagined experience and a real one, so make sure your imaginings are positive as we all need our inner voice to help us navigate the pathways of life. Make a note of all the negative messages you give yourself in a day and try to eliminate them in the future. Instead, congratulate yourself when you have done something well; don't be afraid to praise yourself when you have succeeded in something, however small that something might be. Remember that what you think defines who you are and therefore your destiny.